D0298748

04736376

The Answer

The
Answer

Supercharge the Law of Attraction
and find the secret of true happiness

GLENN HARROLD

This edition first published in Great Britain in 2011 by
Orion Books
an imprint of the Orion Publishing Group Ltd
Orion House, 5 Upper St Martin's Lane,
London WC2H 9EA
An Hachette UK Company

1 3 5 7 9 10 8 6 4 2

A CIP catalogue record for this book
is available from the British Library.

ISBN: 978 1 409 11271 6

Printed in Great Britain by
CPI Group (UK) Ltd, Croydon, CR0 4YY

The Orion Publishing Group's policy is to use papers that are natural,
renewable and recyclable and made from wood grown in sustainable forests.
The logging and manufacturing processes are expected to conform to the
environmental regulations of the country of origin.

Every effort has been made to fulfil requirements with regard to
reproducing copyright material. The author and publisher will be
glad to rectify any omissions at the earliest opportunity.

The author and publishers cannot be held responsible for any actions
that may be take by a reader as a result of any reliance on the information
contained in the text, which is entirely at the reader's own risk.

www.orionbooks.co.uk

*I would like to thank Amanda Harris, Laura Sevier,
Nicola Haslett, Aly Harrold and Marie Williamson
for their help and encouragement
in writing this book.*

Contents

'We are what we think.
All that we are
arises with our thoughts.
With our thoughts,
we make the world.'

BUDDHA

What Makes this Book Special?

Do you know what your heart's desire is but feel you can't obtain it? Are you dissatisfied and frustrated as a result?

The Answer is for you.

 The Law of Attraction

You've probably heard of the Law of Attraction – in essence, that the Universe delivers back to you exactly what you feel about yourself and the world in general.

In other words, you create your own reality by the way you think and feel, and by what you say and do.

There have been a number books on the subject (see page 52 for a brief history) with techniques on how to use the Law of Attraction to attract amazing things into your life.

These techniques follow the same, basic pattern:

- You decide upon a goal. You infuse your goal with positive feelings, imagine it as a reality and regularly project that goal out from within you.

- As a result, you will soon begin to attract opportunities that will enable your goal to actually happen. Using this technique you can make your deepest desires a reality.

Supercharge the process with self-hypnosis

In *The Answer*, I am going to show you how to super-charge this process by combining the Law of Attraction with my self-hypnosis techniques.

When you use the Law of Attraction under hypnosis and you connect with your deepest feelings you will be using the most powerful manifesting energy available to us. (Manifesting in the context of the Law of Attraction is to materialise or make something happen that you have been visualising or imagining.)

The Answer – from the heart

My aim with *The Answer* is to teach you how to use the Law of Attraction from a very heart-centred place so that your projections have a purity to them.

This can be achieved by using self-hypnosis to create a deep state of inner peace.

By using the Law of Attraction in altered states of consciousness you will learn to bypass your ego and connect with your real essence, your spirit or soul.

By projecting your goal from a loving, harmonious place while in a deep state of relaxation you will you will be infusing it with a pure, high vibrational energy. You will manifest things easily and effortlessly.

This is where the real power of the universal Law of Attraction lies.

It is *The Answer*

'There is a difference between knowing the path and walking the path.'

MORPHEUS, *THE MATRIX*

Introduction

People often ask me how I came up with *The Answer...*

For a number of years in the 1980s and early 1990s I made a living as a musician playing my guitar in a duo in pubs, clubs and bars. It was during this time that I would occasionally share the bill with various stage hypnotists.

From my vantage point backstage, I would watch these hypnotists induce trances through verbal suggestion and touch. I found it fascinating, especially when volunteers from the audience followed the most outrageous suggestions seemingly without question.

Although this spectacle sparked my interest in hypnosis, it was the potential of hypnosis to change and heal destructive patterns of behaviour that appealed to me, rather than to entertain.

After passing a two-year diploma course with the London College of Clinical Hypnosis in the early 1990s I became a qualified hypnotherapist. I soon built a busy private practice in my local area and gained great personal satisfaction from helping people overcome their problems.

Since then, I have treated thousands of clients and have dealt with every kind of stress-related problem and all types of phobias. I have helped people to lose weight, stop smoking, overcome fears and phobias, conquer sleep problems, build self-confidence and reach their goals.

After spending a number of years seeing up to 25 clients a week, I drew upon my musical background and began making hypnosis tapes and then later CDs and downloads, primarily to support my work with my clients.

I started by recording tapes at my small home studio, duplicating them one by one, printing off covers and then driving round and selling them to local stores for a £5 each, on a sale-or-return basis.

At the time of writing, my hypnosis CDs, MP3 downloads and iPhone Apps have sold over 1,500,000 copies. My hypnosis Apps have been downloaded 500,000 times in the last 12 months. I have recently helped a number of celebrity clients and some of my sessions have been featured in the UK press and on TV.

However, life hasn't always been easy for me. I grew up in a very dysfunctional household and I responded in a negative way. From the age of 12, I often ran away from home and slept rough on the streets.

At 15, I was expelled from school and at 17, I developed yellow jaundice caused by serious alcohol abuse. My doctor told me that if I didn't quit alcohol I'd be dead in 18 months. I also took drugs, had run-ins with the law and got into lots of scraps.

I don't regret my past, as it has led me to where I am today, but it was not the best start in life. Yet a strong desire to make something of myself and prove my teachers wrong meant that I eventually figured out how to overcome my addictive patterns of behaviour.

Now in my late forties I have been a non-smoker for 20 years, a vegetarian for 10 years and am as fit and healthy as I have ever been. I swim regularly, play tennis three times a week and practise yoga.

I always put my personal and career success down to discovering self-hypnosis and the Law of Attraction. Using both these techniques I learnt to transform my life from the inside out. I knew there had to be a solution and I eventually found it within.

I call this system *The Answer*.

- *The Answer* will show you how to attract anything you desire through the Law of Attraction, and then supercharge your goals with special self-hypnosis techniques.

- *The Answer* will help you achieve your goals and make changes quickly and easily. It worked for me and it will work for you when you follow the steps in this book.

- *The Answer* will give you all of the tools you need to succeed in all areas of your life. My system will show you how to become happier, improve your health and well-being and live a life of abundance. It will show you how to attract unlimited wealth, success and the love of your life. With a little focus and determination you will become empowered on so many levels.

Remember, anything is possible.

The secret to creating an abundant and successful lifestyle is simply to change your inner programming by feeding your mind with positive energy.

The Answer will show you how.

It took me a number of years to learn this but when I did my circumstances changed dramatically and I began to create my own success. I went from being permanently broke and struggling to a life of abundance and opportunity. Because of my journey, this is the book that I have always wanted to write.

I want you to think of this as the beginning of an ongoing journey, where you continually learn, grow and improve the quality of your life.

I hope that *The Answer* helps you fulfil your heart's desire and brings you true happiness.

*'Begin to be now what you
will be hereafter.'*

WILLIAM JAMES

How this Book Works

There are many different ideas and techniques throughout *The Answer* that will help you to use the Law of Attraction to become master of your own destiny and a magnet for success. The core technique is my *ten step system* in chapter 6.

The Answer is divided into two parts.

PART ONE is a general introduction to *The Answer*. The book begins by helping you to focus on what would make you truly happy and to create goals and affirmations.

You'll learn about the Law of Attraction and self-hypnosis, the two elements that make up *The Answer*, before being introduced to *The Answer*'s core technique – *the ten step system*. When you use the system regularly you will be harnessing the full power of the Law of Attraction and you will be able to attract anything you desire.

In further chapters I show you ways to enhance the results and give you some top tips on staying positive. Throughout the chapters there are Take Action exercises and *5 minute wonder techniques* to explore.

PART TWO looks at specific areas of life in which *The Answer* can help give you solutions – health, wealth, love and relationships, career, home environment, stress, fear and the future. Each section is completed with a Take Action exercise.

Finally I end ith a summary: *The Answer*'s 12 golden rules.

The aim of *The Answer* is to help you to reach your true potential and draw out the creativity of your imagination. We are each blessed with the ability to imagine and when we learn how to harness that power we can achieve practically anything.

Using your imagination as such a tool can help you make positive changes to the way you live your life. I sometimes liken the process to planting seeds in the fertile soil of your mind that, with love and attention, will grow into beautiful flowers.

Part One

Happiness

1

What is True Happiness?

'Happiness is the meaning and purpose of life, the
whole aim and end of human existence.'

ARISTOTLE

You know those days when the sun shines, and you've just had a
great meeting at work or an invigorating run around the park.

Or perhaps you've just booked a holiday with the woman or man
of your dreams.

Or something good happens when you least expect it…

You feel happy and you look around and think: 'I love my life, my
home, my job, my friends, my body…'

Your heart sings. Life feels good.

Feeling good

True happiness is about feeling good. For that moment, that day, week
or even that year you are truly happy with who you are and where you
are in life.

You enjoy life as it is.

You enjoy the sense of being alive.

You feel this happiness in your heart.

You cherish those around you more and feel gratitude for loved
ones and friends. This warm glow spreads still further. When you feel

like this you appreciate the sights and colours of the world – the feel of a gentle breeze on your cheek, the rustle of the leaves, the taste of a perfectly ripe cherry.

You have an inner sparkle and a positivity that those around you seem to sense.

> '*Success is not the key to happiness. Happiness is the key to success. If you love what you are doing, you will be successful.*'
>
> HERMAN CAIN

You feel boosted in this state. You value yourself more and with this self-belief, you have the confidence to challenge yourself, to take risks. If, for instance there are things that you do need, such as a pay rise, you are bold enough to ask for them.

Wouldn't life taste sweeter if you felt like this more often?

The daily grind

Of course, most of us feel a whole range of emotions daily: impatience in traffic jams, sadness at the thought of an ill parent or friend or worry about money. Much of the time we feel bored or exhausted by the daily grind.

How we crave those moments when we feel fully alive, energised and lit up from the inside. You recognise that inner glow in others too, like when friends tell you they've got engaged or are expecting a child for instance. It's the glow of true happiness.

The first step

But before we look at *The Answer* in more detail, you need to think deeply about what your personal ingredients of happiness are. Knowing what you want from life is essential before trying out the techniques listed later in the book.

'The Answer will show you how to unlock your inner potential and live a full and happy life.'

What are the ingredients of happiness?

Happiness comes in many forms and blends. Listed below are some obvious ones. . .

Mind and Body

- Peace of mind – freedom from stress.
- Feeling comfortable in your skin.
- Self-confidence and self-belief.
- Good health – for you and your family.
- Energy – physical and mental.
- Positivity – when life gets tough.
- Appreciation and gratitude for what you have.

Relationships

- Creating and being part of a family.
- Love and support – from partners, friends and family.
- A friendly workplace.
- Being part of a thriving community.
- Giving to others – whether kindness, help, time or money.

Leisure and Pleasure

- Balance – having time to socialise, exercise or do the things you love.
- Excitement, passion – doing things that make you feel alive.
- Adventure – exploring the world or taking up new pursuits.
- Treats – a luxury holiday, eating out or a regular massage.
- Variety – not getting stuck in a rut.
- Creating a home – feeling rooted and secure.

A sense of purpose and meaning in life

- Feeling useful to society and the world at large.
- Fulfilment – knowing you're on the right path in life.
- Having a goal or a life path and working your way to achieving it.
- Wealth – or at least financial stability and comfort.
- An ethical or spiritual framework that gives meaning life.

Many of these routes to happiness are universal, others are specific and a question of personal choice. For instance, a free spirit might crave novelty, adventure and adrenaline while a nesting type thrives on security, roots and routine.

Balance

Happiness from the heart

> '*Deep down each of us*
> *knows what makes our*
> *heart sing.*'

Science, religion and philosophy have over the years come up with different definitions of happiness and routes to attaining it. While these can be useful, deep down each of us knows what makes our heart sing. It may be as simple as feeling fit after daily runs on the beach, seeing a child thrive in a school play or cooking a great lasagne for friends.

A state of mind

Happiness is not just about external things – it's also a state of mind. When we don't feel at peace with ourselves and the world, it has a knock-on effect and everything can seem dark or difficult. So for some, happiness is about feeling more calm and relaxed.

Appreciating what you do have

An essential step towards making *The Answer* work for you is to work out what you really want in life.

But before you create your wish list it's helpful to have a sense of gratitude for what you already have.

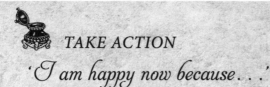

TAKE ACTION

'I am happy now because...'

Get out a pen and paper or a journal and ask yourself the following question:

What makes you truly happy in your life *NOW* as it is?

List everything you can think of including the things you take for granted such as your health.

What becomes clear is that happiness isn't just about getting something you don't have.

Happiness is also about appreciating what you already have.

Knowing what you want

Of course, there might be areas of your life that would like to change or things you would like to attract.

- More money.
- A different job.
- More holiday time.

So this is the fun bit: creating a wish list. Here are two exercises to help you hone in on what you really want.

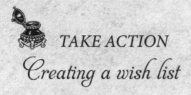

TAKE ACTION
Creating a wish list

Get out a pen and paper or journal and take the time to ask yourself the following:

- What areas of your life would you most like to change?
- What would make you truly happy?

It might be helpful to try the exercise on page 22 first to give you a clear overview of your life so that you can decide what to focus on.

The *wheel of life exercise* helps you to identify how balanced your life is and what needs to be worked on, or changed, in order to create balance and happiness.

Another pull quote here?
Big space otherwise

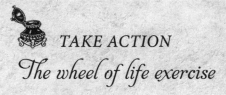

TAKE ACTION
The wheel of life exercise

1. Draw a large circle and split it into eight equal sections.

2. Label the eight sections as follows: Health, Wealth, Family and Friends, Career, Romantic Relationships, Fun and Hobbies, Personal Development, Physical Environment.

3. Imagining that the centre of the circle is 0 and the other edge is 10, rank your level of satisfaction with each area of your life by drawing a curved line to create a new outer edge. Then shade in the section between the centre of the circle and the curved line. For example, if your career was a 10 out of 10 then the whole section would be shaded in.

4. Now look at your wheel, which is a clear overview of your whole life. What do you notice? Have some sections of your life been neglected, which is reflected in their ranking? What areas of your life need some work?

5. Keep the wheel handy when you read chapter 3 on creating goals. So that you can see what areas your goals need to focus on.

6. Repeat this exercise every three months so that you can track your progress.

The ideal situation would be to have every section completely filled, but this just isn't realistic. Instead, the aim is to create a nice balance, not perfection!

In the next chapter we'll look at how to turn your wishes into goals and affirmations.

SUMMARY

- An essential step towards making *The Answer* work for you is to work out what you want in life.

- Happiness is not just about external things – it's also a state of mind.

- True happiness is felt in the heart.

- It's important to have a sense of gratitude for what you already have in life that makes you happy.

- Creating a *wheel of life* (see page 22) helps you identify any imbalances in your life so that you can decide what needs to be worked on or changed in order to create happiness.

'The Answer can help you create more happiness in life by making your wish list become a reality.'

Opportunity

2

Creating Your Goals

'Shoot for the moon. Even if you miss,
you'll land among the stars.'

LES BROWN

Now you've worked out what you want in life it's time to write
down some actual goals.

Setting clear goals is a key element in achieving success. You
wouldn't get on a bus if you didn't know where it was going and the
same applies to your life.

You must have a clear direction and know exactly what you want
to achieve.

*'Always be sure that your goals
are for the good of all concerned and
coming from a place of love.'*

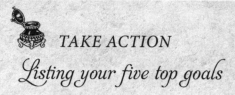

TAKE ACTION
Listing your five top goals

List your five top goals now.

A goal is something that you are setting yourself to achieve. For example, 'I will be in a wonderful, harmonious loving relationship with my ideal partner by August 2013'. Then rewrite them in the present tense.

When you list them in the present tense they become an affirmation:

- I am in a wonderful, harmonious and loving relationship with my ideal partner.
- I am self-employed as a [insert job] with lots of free time.
- I am a confident public speaker.

Top tips on goal writing

- **Be present**. Always use the present tense whenever you write down your goals and affirmations, as if they are a reality now. Even though they may not be a reality now, you are simply programming your mind to believe they are.

- **The sky is the limit**. Don't put a limitation on your goals as the higher you aim the more chance you will have of succeeding.

- **Be specific**. Always be very clear and specific when you state your goals as the Universe will deliver back to you exactly what you affirm. For example, don't say, 'I am going to come into money', as the Universe won't interpret this clearly. It is possible to come into money by having an accident and receiving compensation or through someone passing away.

- **Do it with LOVE**. Always be sure that your goals are for the good of all concerned and coming from a place of love. Your intentions must always be good and honourable.

When you've written down your goals, print them off and put them in places where you will read them each day like the bathroom mirror, next to your PC, or on your fridge. Alternatively, write them on Post-it notes and do the same.

I suggest you always have a top five list of goals.

Once you have achieved one of them replace it with a new one. Update and revise them regularly as your circumstances change.

Step by step

It's important to not only visualise what you want, but to know the steps you need to take to get there.

Creating a simple *ladder of happiness* (see page 30) will help you to set realistic goals and outline a step by step process to achieve them.

Depending on your goal, ladders may have more or fewer steps. It doesn't matter how many steps the ladder has, just do what works for you.

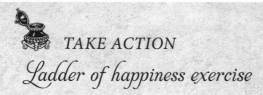

TAKE ACTION

Ladder of happiness exercise

1. Set yourself a goal. By all means be realistic, but don't limit yourself in any way because in the Law of Attraction anything is possible.

2. Draw a ladder consisting of five steps and at the top of the ladder label your desired goal. For example, if your goal is to find a loving relationship, then at the top write something like 'a beautiful, loving romantic relationship.'

3. Now imagine that the bottom of the ladder is where you are now. What steps do you need to take to get to the top of the ladder and achieve your goal? Goals don't always have to be external; they can be about making changes inside you too.

4. If you find it difficult to know what steps you need to take, then it can help to talk to friends and family who have achieved your desired goal and be open to any insight they have.

5. Hang the ladder where you will see it every day, or at least regularly. When you complete a step you may like to mark it with a gold star so that you can track, and feel good about, the progress you are making.

A beautiful, loving,
romantic relatonship

Try different
ways of meeting
potential partners
ie internet
dating

Have the
courage to try
new things and go
to different places

Put more time
aside for socialising
and meeting new
people

Let go of past hurt so
I can welcome a new
relationship

Decide what
I want from a
partner

When you set goals and take the necessary action to achieve them, you are telling the Universe that you are serious about your dreams and serious about making them a reality.

So, now you have your goals lined up. In the next chapter I'll tell you more about *The Answer*, a technique that will help you manifest your dream life based on your goals. So dream on. . .

SUMMARY

- Setting clear, specific goals is a key element in achieving success.

- Always use the present tense whenever you write down your goals and affirmations.

- Don't put a limitation on your goals.

- Always be sure that your goals are for the good of all.

- Write your goals down and read them everyday.

- Creating a *ladder of happiness* will help you to set realistic goals and outline a step by step process to achieve them.

'If you can dream it,
you can do it.'

WALT DISNEY

Faith

3

What is The Answer?

'Be careful what you wish for, it might just come true...'

PROVERB

So, now that you've honed in on what would make you truly happy and written your goals I'm going to introduce you to

The Answer

The Answer is simple:

You already have the power and potential within you to be truly happy, whatever happiness means to you.

Whether it's having more money, being successful in your work, losing weight and getting fit, becoming less stressed or all of these things, The Answer can help you.

It doesn't matter what background, education or qualifications you have, anyone can change their life, for the better.

With the right knowledge, some new positive programming and a little hard work, success and happiness can be achieved by anyone.

Think positive

I know the term 'positive programming' is a little technical, yet I believe the mind is a like a computer – what you put in is what will come back out.

By feeding your mind with positive energy through positive affirmations and visualisations you will begin to have mastery over your life. When you do this in a state of self-hypnosis it will have a deeper and longer lasting effect.

This is the real secret to feeling emotionally balanced, more positive, reducing stress and anxiety, being at your sharpest and best when you need to be and so much more.

When you learn to take control of your thoughts you will have more control of your emotions and you will feel happier.

The Answer will show you how.

The technique

For 20 years I've been using a special technique to create the life I've always wanted to live and I've helped many others do the same.

That technique, which I've called *The Answer*, is made of two integral elements:

1. The Law of Attraction

The first is the Law of Attraction, which can be simply described as:

> *'Whatever your give your attention and focus to, you will attract into your life.'*

So whether you want a new lover, a change of home or a new career, if you work with the Law of Attraction you can achieve all kinds of goals.

In chapter 4 I'll go into more detail about how this law works and teach you how you can use it to make your dreams a reality.

 2. Self-hypnosis

The second is self-hypnosis, which can simply be described as:

> *'The ability to focus your mind intently on a goal while in a relaxed state of mind and body.'*

As a hypnotherapist with 20 years experience I have literally seen miracles when working with clients.

Self-hypnosis is something anyone can do and when you incorporate it into your daily routines it will transform your life. In chapter 5 I'll tell you more about self-hypnosis.

The Answer

> *'When you use self-whypnosis in combination with the Law of Attraction the effects are turbo charged.'*

The Answer

= 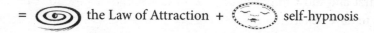 the Law of Attraction + self-hypnosis

Let me explain. When you focus on a goal and you project it out into the Universe you are using the energy of the Law of Attraction.

When you do the same thing in a state of self-hypnosis you are using a much greater part of your mind and the energy you create will have more depth and power.

By engaging your unconscious mind you will draw upon hidden pools of creativity and utilise your heart energy.

As a result, the manifestation of your goal will be bigger and more complete and it will also come back to you more quickly if that is what you need.

The importance of belief

> '*You have within you all the tools
> you need to create the life you want.*'

Before you embark on the techniques I give you in *The Answer*, you have to take a leap of faith.

The first and most important factor in changing your life for the better is to have belief.

Most people's inner beliefs hold them back and stop them achieving any sort of success.

If you believe that only others become successful or that life is a struggle or you don't deserve good things, then you will have little chance of achieving your heart's desire.

You have to change destructive, negative beliefs and take consistent, positive action towards your goals.

Living the dream

You need to create a thought process whereby every cell in your mind and body believes that you are living your dream life NOW – even if your bank statement says otherwise.

Create the belief first and you will soon manifest the reality.

The key to success is to understand that you have within you all the tools you need to create the life you want.

Belief

Living a dream life with a perfect partner/job/home and lots of money is not down to luck, it is the result of hard work, diligence and planning.

The Answer will teach you how to create your own luck and become luckier all the time.

TAKE ACTION
Belief and abundance technique

Self-hypnosis is a fast way to change negative thought patterns. Here is a simple technique that will get you off to a good start and will help you begin to believe that you deserve all the good life has to offer.

- **Close your eyes and take a few slow, deep, rhythmical breaths**. Breathe in through your nose and out through your mouth in a circular breathing motion.

- **Calm your mind** as you continue to breathe slowly, rhythmically and deeply. After a few minutes you will begin to feel centred.

- **In this relaxed state**, believe that you deserve to live a life that is abundant, happy, full of love and joy. Connect with a strong belief that you deserve the very best life has to offer and feel it resonate through every cell in your mind and body.

- **Feel your self letting go of any negative beliefs** or old conditioning around living a full, successful and happy life. Repeat to yourself, slowly and steadily, the following words over and over in a slow, steady mantra:
  'I deserve to be happy, healthy, wealthy and abundant.'

- **Really FEEL it** as you repeat the words. Feel happy and joyful and let these feelings grow stronger as you progress and get deeper into it. Do this for 10–15 minutes, or longer if you prefer.

In the following two chapters we're going to look at the two vital components of *The Answer* in more detail. First up in chapter 4, the Law of Attraction. . .

SUMMARY

- By feeding your mind with positive energy through positive affirmations and visualisations you will begin to have mastery over your life.

- When you do this in a state of self-hypnosis it will have a deeper and longer lasting effect.

- *The Answer* is made of two integral elements:

  the Law of Attraction and   self-hypnosis

- When you use self-hypnosis in combination with the Law of Attraction the effects are turbo charged.

- Through hypnosis, you engage your unconscious mind and will draw upon hidden pools of creativity and utilise your heart energy.

- The first and most important factor in changing your life for the better is to have belief.

- You have to change destructive, negative beliefs and take consistent, positive action towards your goals.

- You need to create a thought process whereby every cell in your mind and body believes that you are living your dream life NOW.

Desire

4
The Power of the Law of Attraction

'What the mind of man can conceive
and believe, it can achieve.'

NAPOLEON HILL

In the previous chapter we looked at the two key components of *The Answer*: the Law of Attraction  and self-hypnosis  along with the importance of belief.

In this chapter we're going to take a brief look at the Law of Attraction.

- What is the Law of Attraction and how does it work?
- How can it help me live a happier more fulfilled life?

The Answer

Introducing. . . the Law of Attraction

There are many different universal laws that affect the way that we live and interact with our world. Some of these universal laws are better understood than others.

We now fully accept and understand the law of gravity but up until Isaac Newton discovered it in the late 17th century we were ignorant of it.

The universal Law of Attraction is one of these laws. It affects all of us all and has been with us since the beginning of time (see the box on page 52).

However, whereas the law of gravity is a scientific fact, the Law of Attraction falls into the belief category. It is only understood by those who *believe* in it or who those who use it to their advantage.

> *'The universal Law of Attraction is simple: what you give out will come back to you.'*

So what is it?

When you make a statement with feeling and intent behind it the Law Of Attraction will respond.

Whever thoughts you think and feelings you feel will determine what you attract back into your life.

When you make a statement with feeling and intent behind it the Law Of Attraction will respond.

So if you say: 'I feel good' you are creating energy. If you affirm regularly that you feel good, your energy will build and you will find yourself in situations that make you feel good.

The key is to have a crystal clear intention and to energise this intention completely so that every cell and fibre in your mind and body is resonating with it. Then project it out to the Universe.

In *The Answer* I will show you how to do this on many different levels.

Law of Attraction case study

Nicola, 23, first heard about the Law of Attraction a few years ago. She decided to try it for herself on somewthing small to see if it really worked.

One evening, a few hours before travelling to London she asked the Universe for a free travel card. She visualised coming across a free ticket and having a safe journey and then put out the request to the Universe and let it go.

That evening as she stood by the ticket machine about to pay for her ticket a woman behind her said, 'Would you like a free travel card? I don't need it anymore'. Every ticket machine that evening was occupied and yet the woman chose to give it to her. She realised in that moment howw powerful the Law of Attraction was.

She went on to manifest some amazing things in her life. She is now a successful Harley Street hypnotherapist and she coaches people on the Law of Attraction.

'Energise your intention
completely so that every cell
and fibre in your mind and body
is resonating with it.'

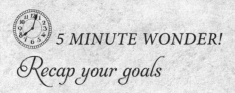

5 MINUTE WONDER!

Recap your goals

When you are in the shower, travelling somewhere, having lunch, in a queue or waiting around, spend five minutes recapping your top five goals. Think about them and connect with feelings of happiness and joy as you see them becoming a reality.

Use any spare time in your day to recap your goals so that you strengthen the energy of them, especially by using your feelings.

The science

As I mentioned earlier, the Law of Attraction is more of a belief system than hard science. However, there have been a number of scientific studies that show how our inner thoughts and feelings impact the world around us. One such study is how our thoughts and feelings affect water.

How water responds to love

Dr Masaru Emoto, a Japanese scientist, discovered that when water is exposed to loving words or uplifting music the crystals formed in the frozen water revealed brilliant, complex, and colourful snowflake patterns.

In contrast, water exposed to negative thoughts, music and energy, froze into crystals with incomplete, asymmetrical patterns in dull colours.

Intention

The effect of these studies is groundbreaking. Our body is three-quarters water and half of the Earth is made up of water.

Nice vibes

Quantum physics maintains that everything in the Universe is a mass of molecules and atoms vibrating at certain frequencies.

We all have a vibrational energy that we emit. Our energy field impacts the way that our outer world reacts to us. If you remain in a space of love, peace, happiness then that is what will manifest in your outer world.

Your vibrational energy is determined by your thoughts, feelings and lifestyle. If you sleep well, eat healthily, exercise regularly, watch, read and listen to uplifting, positive things then your vibrational energy will be strong. On page 96 I explain more about how to do this.

Attract or repel

Many people are already unconsciously using the Law Of Attraction without realising it.

Think of the times when you have met someone by chance and as a result your life totally changed. Perhaps lots of new opportunities came from that meeting. If a chance meeting created problems and difficulties it will also be because of what you were feeling and emitting.

Our vibrational energy will align us with other people and situations of a similar energy.

This is why you can meet someone for the first time and feel very in tune with them without really knowing them at all. It can also work in the reverse when you feel repelled by someone you meet with a very different energy to yourself.

Resonating with and projecting positive energy will always put you in the right place at the right time.

To believe or not to believe

A short history of the Law of Attraction

- The Law of Attraction, also known as 'Cosmic Ordering' goes back a long way. The terms used to describe the phenomena have changed over the years, but the principles of it can be found in old manuscripts. There is a quote, often used, from the Bible: 'Ask and it will be given to you; seek, and you will find; knock, and it will be opened to you' *(Luke 11.9)*.

- The words 'Law of Attraction' can be traced back to 1879 when they first appeared in print in the *New York Times*. During this time in the 19th century 'New Thought Writers' emerged and presented lectures about the Law of Attraction, its principles and how it could be applied to daily life. One such writer was Thomas Troward. His work inspired many other New Thought Writers.

- In 1906 *Thought Vibration or The Law of Attraction in the Thought World* was written by William Walker. The book describes how our negative and positive thoughts affect our physical world and so shape our lives.

- Wallace D. Wattles's book *The Science of Getting Rich* published in 1910 highlights the Hindu principles of the Law of Attraction and conveys the idea that God can deliver everything we ask of him.

- 'What the mind of man can conceive and believe, it can achieve.' These are the words of American author Napoleon Hill who is considered to be one of the great writers on success. His most famous book *Think and Grow Rich* was published in 1937 has sold more than 60 million copies to date. Hill helped people to understand how powerful their own thoughts are and that by harnessing positive thought patterns they could attract anything they desired.

- Other authors like Dr Norman Vincent Peale followed on with these ideas. Peale's most famous book *The Power of Positive Thinking* (2003) can still be found today in any self-help section of a good bookshop.

- The basic principles of the Law of Attraction, or Cosmic Ordering have been rewritten and made new to appeal to new readers and changing attitudes. The first book with the words Cosmic Order in the actual title was written by German author Bärbel Mohr in 1995. The book *The Cosmic Ordering Service* is now published in 14 languages with over 1.5 million copies in print.

- The Law of Attraction and Cosmic Ordering have become prominent in the media in the last ten years with celebrity endorsement from people like Noel Edmunds and Jonathan Cainer. A number of books were published on the subject around the same time.

- One of the most successful films and books on the theme of the Law of Attraction is Rhonda Byrne's *The Secret*. The author was so influenced by *The Science of Getting Rich* by Wallace D. Wattles that she read countless books along the same theme, researched many old manuscripts and finally came to write *The Secret*. The book was written after the release of the film and has been translated into 44 languages with over 21 million copies in print.

The Law of Attraction has divided opinion for a long time now. Sceptics and critics will point to young children who develop terrible diseases as an example that the law is flawed.

I have no definitive answers to these deep moral and philosophical questions and if anyone tries to tell you they have, forget it. I believe brain power alone is limited in its understanding of the Universe and its many mysteries.

I never try to convert sceptics, and I always respect others' opinions.

But I can tell you that when you use the Law of Attraction to attract more love, abundance, opportunity and happiness it works every time.

There is a benevolent, loving energy out there in the Universe that can help you improve the quality of your life. It has completely transformed my life and I wouldn't be writing this book without it.

The Answer is about giving people tools to achieve success rather than justifying every aspect of the Law of Attraction. So take what you want from *The Answer* and make it work for you.

*'For those who believe, no explanation
is necessary. For those who do not, none
will suffice.'*

JOSEPH DUNNINGER

SUMMARY

- The universal Law of Attraction is only understood by those who *believe* in it or who those who use it to their advantage.

- The Law of Attraction is simple: whatever thoughts you think and feelings you feel will determine what you attract back into your life.

- The key is to have a crystal clear intention and to energise this intention completely so that every cell and fibre in your mind and body is resonating with it. Then project it out to the Universe.

- If you remain in a space of love, peace and happiness then that is what will manifest in your outer world.

- Your vibrational energy will align you with other people and situations of a similar energy. Resonating with and projecting positive energy will always put you in the right place at the right time.

- Spend five minutes everyday recapping your top five goals and affirmations.

- *The Answer* will show you how to supercharge the Law of Attraction with self-hypnosis.

Relax

5

The Power of Self-Hypnosis

'The more man meditates upon good thoughts, the
better will be his world and the world at large.'

CONFUCIUS

Now we've looked at the first element of *The Answer*, the Law of
Attraction, it's time to supercharge it with self-hypnosis.
In this chapter you'll learn:

- How easy it is hypnotise yourself.
- How hypnosis helps get you into the optimum state for focusing on
  your goals.

Then in the next chapter things really get exciting as you get to try the
core technique of *The Answer* – the *ten step system*.

A word about hypnosis

Self-hypnosis sounds more complicated than it is. It is also completely safe when you follow the guidelines and techniques in this book.

Self-hypnosis is simply the ability to focus your attention on a goal while in a state of relaxation.

When you experience it you are simply in an altered state of consciousness. Being in a trance is something you have experienced naturally many times in your life. Daydreaming is a naturally occurring trance state, as is the moment in-between being asleep and fully awake.

In *The Answer* you'll learn how to create those states at will to empower yourself in many different ways.

When you're in a self-induced or naturally occurring trance you will be more receptive to accepting suggestions because your unconscious mind is more open and receptive at this time.

How it works

In a typical hypnosis session your brainwaves will actually slow down as you go deeper into a trance, and then speed up as you come out of the trance.

This also occurs naturally when you go to sleep each night, then conversely when you awaken in the morning. These brain cycle states are referred to as the beta, alpha, theta and delta states. The alpha and theta states are our bridge to the unconscious.

Relaxed. . .

When we go into the *alpha* state our brain cycles slow down to between nine to 14 cycles per second. This is achieved through relaxation or light meditation where you are still aware of everything around you but your mind is calm and you are feeling physically relaxed.

Deeply relaxed. . .

When we go into the *theta* state our brain cycles slow down to 5–8 cycles a second. At this point you are in a deep state of hypnosis. In both the alpha and theta states we become very receptive to hypnotic suggestion that can be acted upon.

Supercharging your goals

When you use self-hypnosis to supercharge the goals you wrote in chapter 2 you will build a very powerful energy, especially when you induce strong feelings in a deep state of relaxation.

This is the optimum state for focusing on your goals as when we go into self-hypnosis or meditation we access the right hemisphere of the brain. The right side is where your creativity lies and through hypnosis you will be tapping into the infinite, universal source of creativity that is available to us all.

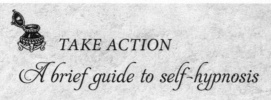

TAKE ACTION
A brief guide to self-hypnosis

Below is the basic self-hypnosis technique. Try it to familiarise yourself with the process…

1. **Create a quiet atmosphere**. Find a quiet room where you will not be disturbed. Turn of your phone and dim the lights. Make yourself comfortable, either sitting in a chair with a headrest or lying on a bed or sofa.

2. **Prepare yourself**. Tell yourself silently or out loud that you're going to practice self-hypnosis and how long you want to remain in a trance. 15–20 minutes is fine to begin with although after a few weeks practice you may want to make your session last longer.

3. **The breathing technique**. Close your eyes and begin to breathe from your diaphragm (lower chest area) and not from the upper chest. If you are breathing properly your chest will go out as you breathe in and go in as you breathe out. You can also say the word relax on every out-breath if you wish. Continue focusing on this breathing pattern ten or more times – or for as long as it takes for you to feel completely relaxed.

4. **Clearing your mind**. Allow your mind to go completely blank. Don't worry if you get unwanted thoughts drifting into your mind. One useful method is to imagine a clear blue sky on a summer's day. Imagine any thoughts that pop up as clouds that then fade away leaving the sky clear and blue again.

5. **Deepening the trance state**. By now you're in a light trance state. A good technique to guide yourself deeper is to count down (silently and slowly) from ten to one. Feel every muscle in your body relax more and more with each descending number.

6. **Utilising the trance state**. When you reach the deeper trance you can either relax and drift off or you can give yourself some positive suggestions or affirmations. Choose a goal you wrote in chapter 2. Work on only one goal at a time, usually over a number of sessions. Really feel the affirmations as you repeat them. Say them with complete conviction.

7. **Wake up**. When you feel it's time to wake up from the trance just slowly count up from one to ten. Tell yourself you're becoming more awake with each number. When you reach the number ten your eyes will be open and you'll be wide-awake enjoying a feeling of total well-being.

Don't worry. . .

. . . if you feel you're not deep enough in trance or nothing is happening. Being in a trance is often very subtle. The more you practice, the better you will get.

. . . about going into a deep state of trance, as this takes you to a powerful part of yourself where you make big changes. Allow yourself to go deep into your mind and tell yourself you feel safe and secure as you do this. You cannot get stuck in a trance state.

. . . if you fall asleep – you will then wake up in your own time as you would from a regular sleep state.

Case study on writing a number one hit

Lucinda Drayton is a talented singer and songwriter who wrote and sang the Bliss song 'One Hundred Thousand Angels'. She also wrote a number one hit in the mid-Nineties.

She told me told me that when she learnt about self-hypnosis and the power of affirmations she would regularly affirm that she would have a number one hit. Every day she would get herself into a very centred state and affirm and visualise this scenario in colourful detail. She also wrote the affirmations down 40 times and worked on reprogramming her unconscious through hypnosis.

She explained that hypnosis helped her to remove negative blocks and raise her vibration so that attracting the goal became effortless. When using self-hypnosis she really used her feelings to imagine having the number one hit.

Within one year of starting this discipline in the mid-Nineties, she wrote a song with her partner that went to number one in the British charts.

Self-hypnosis: tapping into the Earth's frequency?

The great scientist and humanitarian Nikola Tesla discovered that the resonant frequency of the Earth is approximately 8Hz (hertz). He made this discovery while transmitting extremely low frequencies through the ground while he researched ways to transmit energy wirelessly over long distances.

Interestingly, theta brain waves also cycle in this range and it is the theta state that we enter when we are in self-hypnosis.

When we project our affirmations and goals while in the theta state maybe we are also harnessing some of the Earth's natural energy, which is why using the Law Of Attraction in a state of self-hypnosis is so powerful and effective.

If our brain cycles are in synch with the resonant frequency of Earth when we project our goals, we are drawing on some very powerful natural energy.

So believe in these techniques, because anything you want is just waiting for you to step up and claim it.

'When you use self-hypnosis to supercharge your goals you will build a very powerful energy.'

SUMMARY

- Self-hypnosis is simply the ability to focus your attention on a goal while in a state of relaxation.

- Daydreaming is a naturally occurring trance state, as is the moment in-between being asleep and fully awake.

- In *The Answer* you'll learn how to create those states at will to empower yourself in many different ways.

- When you're in a self-induced or naturally occurring trance you will be more receptive to accepting suggestions because your unconscious mind is more open and receptive at this time.

- When you use self-hypnosis to supercharge the goals you wrote in chapter 2 you will build a very powerful energy, especially when you induce strong feelings in a deep state of relaxation.

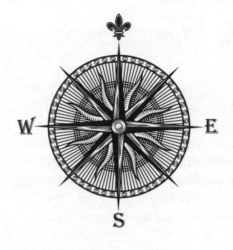

Focus

6

How to Use The Answer: the Ten Step System

Now it's time to really try out *The Answer*.
When using this *ten step system* it is best to focus your energy on a single specific goal.

What is your priority? Think of something that will make your life richer and more fulfilling, whether a soul mate or a new career venture.

The first six steps will help you to focus intently while in a state of self-hypnosis and to use the Law Of Attraction to attract anything that you desire.

The final four steps of the system give you the actions to take in daily life.

So, here goes. . .

STEP 1 – Relax your body and centre your mind

- **Go to a quiet room** where you will not be disturbed, preferably a bedroom with no telephone or a quiet place with no distractions. Dim the lights or turn them off.

- **Close your eyes and breathe very slowly and deeply** in through your nose and out through your mouth. Continue building a very slow and very deep rhythmical breathing pattern. Make sure you breathe from your diaphragm (lower chest area) and not from the upper chest. Continue focusing on this breathing pattern ten or more times, or for as long as it takes for you to feel pleasantly relaxed.

- **Allow your mind to go completely blank**. Don't worry if you still get unwanted thoughts drifting into your mind; tell yourself not to fight them as they will soon drift away again.

- **If you get an unwanted thought**, imagine you are looking up at the sky on a pleasant summer's day. You notice a few small clouds that drift across the sky and then fade away. Eventually all of the clouds have drifted away and the sky is clear. Imagine your conscious thoughts are like clouds that fade away.

The state you are aiming to create is one of strong focus where you are deeply relaxed and your mind is calm and not actually thinking.

With practice you will find it easy to block out distractions and still be able to focus your mind intently.

STEP 2 – Attitude of gratitude

Before you start focusing on your goal. . .

- Think about all the things in your life you are grateful for.
- Now send out a genuine feeling of gratitude for all of these blessings.
- **Take a few minutes to open your heart** and project a strong feeling of gratitude out into the Universe.

STEP 3 – Connecting with the Law of Attraction

- **Imagine the Law of Attraction for a minute**. What does it look like to you? Do you see it as a ball of energy or a matrix? However it looks and feels to you is right.

- **Feel a strong connection** to the universal Law of Attraction.

STEP 4 – Projecting your goal

- **Now focus on your goal and project it** out from within you. Imagine you are sending your goal out into the Universe. Be strong and clear with your intention now.

- **As you do this connect with feelings of happiness and joy**. Breathe slowly, rhythmically and deeply. Build a strong energy through your thoughts and feelings.

- **Allow yourself to go deeper**. Project your goal strongly from your heart and induce feelings of love.

STEP 5 – Clarify your goal

- **Give your goal more colour and detail** as it is important to be very specific. If for example you want to attract the love of your life, think about the qualities you would like this person to have for a happy and fulfilling relationship.

- If your goal is that you want to be financially comfortable, you need to be crystal clear about how you are going to attract the money towards you. You could inherit it or win it, which may not give you the same satisfaction as making it yourself.

STEP 6 – Imagine it as a success NOW

After projecting your goal and building strong positive feelings. . .

- **Imagine your goal is a reality now.** So if your goal is to be with your ideal partner imagine being with them now. See yourself doing all the things you long to do with a partner. Most importantly see yourself in a loving, heart-centred, empowering relationship and imagine it in the present tense.

- Imagining that your goal has already happened will prime your mind to manifest your goal more quickly and easily. This is because when you believe it is a reality now, you will impact your outer reality to attract to you the things you need to achieve this goal in its entirety. You will be aligning yourself with opportunity.

- **Keep focused** on your goal and connected strongly to the Law of Attraction.

- **To wake up**, when you feel ready, take a few breaths and open your eyes and come wide awake. If you are using the system at night time you can drift off to sleep.

That's it! That is the real secret to attracting the things you want into your life. Use this self-hypnosis technique as often as possible. Once a day is ideal so that you build a strong energy that grows over time.

STEP 7 – Feel it

The next three steps are things to do in your every day life.

- **Each day FEEL your goal getting closer**. Whenever you think about it, feel it too. Adding positive, loving feelings is the key element to strengthen your goal. Feel good about having more money, feel happy about being in love.

- Infuse every aspect of your goal with positive feelings of love, joy, happiness and gratitude.

STEP 8 – Take action

It is vital to take action after setting your goal. The Universe will need a little help from you so that it can turn your goal into a reality.

So if you're looking for your perfect partner, you need to get out and about. Put yourself in situations where your chances of meeting your soul mate are good.

'It is very important to clarify that whatever you want to attract comes to you with the highest good of all concerned.'

Action

Join new groups or clubs, broaden your social circle so that you are giving yourself every chance of being in the right place so that he/she can show up. But remember to relax, don't push it.

Project your goal, start to take action and allow it to come to you free of any stress, doubt or worry.

STEP 9 – Write it down

Write your goal down, and then list a number of affirmations that are relevant. For example:

I have a loving romantic relationship with my perfect partner.
I am rich and successful now.

Print them off and put them in places where you will see them every day. Have them by your bathroom mirror, by your bedside, on your PC as a screensaver, on your phone, in your car and so on.

Live, breathe and focus on your goal every day. Use the self-hypnosis technique in this system and you will be amazed at how quickly you will manifest your goal.

STEP 10 – Let go of attachment

Once you have set your goals let go of any attachment to the outcome.

If you think of all the things you desire in your personal life it is only attachment to outcomes that causes misery and stress.

- By accepting all possible outcomes you won't feel any anguish or pain if you are rejected. What will be will be.

- If you set your goals, regularly use the Law of Attraction through the techniques in this book and accept every possible outcome as the right one you will be staying in your own power.

Case study on letting go of attachment

Years ago when I didn't have much money I put a picture of a new Aston Martin in my PC and I visualised owning it. I did this visualisation a number of times and then let go of it. Years later I rediscovered the picture of the Aston a week before I actually bought one.

Eventually that dream became a reality.

That said, I don't have any real attachment to it. It is just something that I enjoy driving at this moment in time. I have just got back from Australia where I spent three months getting around on a very basic little motor scooter that a friend lent me. The scooter and the Aston both do the same job and I felt equally happy driving both.

- When you remain in your own power you build an inner strength that has a magnetism that will help you attract more easily.

- Yearning, longing or hoping things work out for you are weaknesses. It is only normal to experience this kind of thinking from time to time but when you recognise these thoughts let them go and focus your energy on the techniques described in *The Answer*.

- There is a big difference between *wishing* you owned a house by the beach to *visualising and projecting a picture* of yourself owning one but being free of any attachment to it in a material sense.

When you can learn to let go of attachment to outcomes you will become very liberated and empowered.

So project your goal into the Universe with love then let it go. Trust that everything will work out at the right time.

'Live, breathe and focus on your goal every day. Use the self-hypnosis techniques in this system and you will be amazed at how quickly you will manifest your goal.'

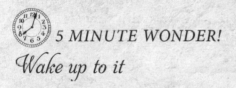 5 MINUTE WONDER!

Wake up to it

Before you wake up in the morning you enter a hypnotic trance state called the hypnopompic state. This naturally occurring trance between sleep and being fully awake is when you will begin to recall dreams and start to become aware of where you are and what you have to do today.

In the hypnopompic state you are highly receptive to suggestions and so it is perfect for focusing on attracting things into your life.

- **As you start to wake up** allow yourself to drift back into the semi-sleep state.

- **Start to focus on your goal**. Really feel it happening and imagine it's a reality. Connect with strong feelings of love, happiness and joy as you do it.

- **Finish by affirming you are going to have a great day** and that you'll overcome any hurdles or challenges.

- **Do this every morning** for five minutes or more and really enjoy it as you do it. Then when you are ready you can emerge from your bed ready to take on the world.

- **Go to sleep to it**. The other ideal time to focus on your goals is just before you go to sleep at night. The time between being awake and going to sleep is also a hypnopompic state.

When you get into this morning or night time manifestation habit you will build a powerful magnetic energy. It will change your life.

You can either use the technique to focus on a specific goal or more generally by imagining all the things you want to make yourself happy.

Remember, the more energy you give to your goal the more spectacularly it will manifest. There are no limitations. Believing is achieving!

SUMMARY

- When using *The Answer's ten step system* it is best to focus your energy on a single specific goal.

- STEP 1 – Relax your body and centre your mind.

- STEP 2 – Open your heart and project a strong feeling of gratitude for all the things in your life you are grateful for out into the Universe.

- STEP 3 – Feel a strong connection to the Universal Law of Attraction.

- STEP 4 – Project your goal strongly from your heart, and induce feelings of love.

- STEP 5 – Clarify your goal – give your goal more colour and detail

- STEP 6 – Imagine it as a success NOW.

- STEP 7 – Each day FEEL your goal getting closer.

- STEP 8 – Take action – get out and about, put yourself in the right places and so on.

- STEP 9 – Write your goal down, and list a number of affirmations that are relevant. Live, breathe and focus on your goal every day and use the self-hypnosis technique described in steps 1–6.

- STEP 10 – Let go of attachment – project your goal into the Universe with love then let it go. Trust that everything will work out at the right time.

- Focus on your goal as you're waking up and going to sleep.

Perspective

7

Top Tips on Positive Thinking

'Attitude is a little thing that makes a big difference.'

WINSTON CHURCHILL

So now you've discovered the how *The Answer* works and what the *ten step system* can do for you, it's time to really zoom in on one crucial element in making *The Answer* work for you.

The importance of thinking positive

Often during the day our minds can drift off and before we know it we're thinking negatively. Watching a few adverts on TV is enough to trigger off a torrent of thoughts such as:

'I wish I looked younger and had legs like that.'
'I hate being stuck in this ugly flat.'
'I'll never be able to afford that car.'

According to the Law of Attraction, whatever you focus on will become a reality so you need to build strategies to minimise negative thinking and worry. Generate as many positive thoughts and feelings as possible.

Everything begins with a thought

When you train your mind to flip negative thoughts and feelings into positive ones you will attract situations towards you that help bring you love, abundance and happiness in all areas of your life. This energy is so powerful and it is available to all of us.

Happiness as a state of mind

*'Happiness is not the absence of problems
but the ability to deal with them.'*

ANON

We are what we think.

Sometimes all you need is a shift in the way you think. Changing your perspective makes you look around and see things in a different light.

Perhaps you realise that it's your negative thinking or fear that is bringing you down, not the situation itself.

The Answer can:

- Help transform your thinking from negative to positive.
- Help you to feel more positive in general.

Opposite are eight top tips on how to become more positive.

How to be more positive

TIP 1 – *See through positive eyes*

To attract more positive things into your life you need to constantly see the world through positive eyes.

Everything is about perspective.

Two people can experience the same situation and respond very differently. Life will always throw up challenges but how you react is up to you.

If you face difficulties with courage and self-belief and force yourself to be more positive it will soon become a habit and you will react more positively when life gets tough.

This is how you turn the tide and start attracting what you want. You will start to create your life and master your destiny rather than being a victim of circumstance.

'You need to build strategies to minimise negative thinking, fear and worry. Generate as many positive thoughts and feelings as possible.'

'Happiness is an attitude. We either make ourselves miserable, or happy and strong. The amount of work is the same.'

FRANCESCA REIGLER

TIP 2 – *Set yourself new challenges*

Step out of your comfort zone by taking on new challenges or confronting any fears you may have. Take small steps if you need to at first but always push yourself.

It may by signing up for a marathon or climbing Mount Kilamanjaro. Or it could be learning a new language or going on that blind date.

Taking on a new challenge gives you a sense of empowerment and will inspire you to achieve many more goals.

It will also build your self-belief and confidence. Why not combine a challenge with raising money for charity, as this will give you added motivation to succeed.

'If you don't like something change it; if you can't change it, change the way you think about it.'

MARY ENGELBREIT

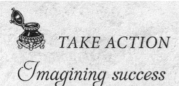

TAKE ACTION
Imagining success

To help you succeed with any challenge you take on, visualise it beforehand in a 100 per cent positive light. Close your eyes and relax your mind and body through deep breathing. Then imagine a movie of the whole event running from start to finish and see it being a very positive experience. Make this movie big and bright and very clear in your mind. If it seems scary, just breathe away any fear or trepidation.

Visualise it every day in the run up to the event and you will feel fantastic when you do it for real.

TIP 3 – *Flip negative thoughts into positive ones*

Get into the habit of thinking positively by being more aware of your thought patterns.

When you notice a negative thought, flip it. Change it immediately into something more positive that makes you feel good. Think of a loved one, listen to an uplifting piece of music or look at one of your favourite photographs.

A positive thought is much more powerful than a negative thought.

Whenever you see the glass half empty instead of half full, change your thinking fast. Instead of focusing on what is wrong in your life, focus now on all the things that are right, that work for you.

TIP 4 – *How are you feeling?*

If you aren't sure whether you are thinking positively or negatively, take note of how you are feeling.

Are you feeling happy? Content?

Good!

Or are you feeling anxious? Worried?

Then look at the thoughts behind your feelings and then CHANGE them. You always have the ability to choose your thoughts.

TIP 5 – *Be selective about what you absorb*

Try to avoid trashy TV and negative stories in the media. What we watch and read impacts our thinking more than we realise.

Be wary of adverts that use clever tactics to influence you to sell you that miracle face cream, 'must have' bag or brand new car.

It's hardly surprising ads like this trigger off bouts of negative thinking when we compare ourselves to the perfect looking (airbrushed) women and men in the images.

'I had the blues because I had no shoes until upon the street, I met a man who had no feet.'

ANCIENT PERSIAN SAYING

5 MINUTE WONDER!

Smile and the world smiles with you

Spend five minutes a day making a conscious effort to smile – it really does work and the response from others will nearly always be uplifting! Smile to yourself and smile at others. If you wake up feeling grumpy for whatever reason make a point of smiling at the first person you see that day.

TIP 6 – *Gratitude*

Gratitude is a very good way to flip out of negative thinking and feel more positive.

Start to think about the things in your life that you are grateful for.

Your home, friends, family, children, pets, your healthy body, clothes, books, music, hobbies, talents, your ability to laugh and have fun and so on.

Think of all the things you are grateful for right now.

If you have perfect use of your arms and legs and the ability to walk, run, read, write, hear, see and talk, then you are lucky. If you are healthy in mind and body, take a moment to give thanks for that. Never take your health, happiness and well-being for granted.

Gratitude

Make a point on waking each morning of focusing on all the blessings in your life.

When you are feeling grateful, you are in a positive state. Feeling grateful means that you are creating more things to be grateful about. That is how the Law of Attraction works.

TIP 7 – *Feel love*

'Love is the only sane and satisfactory answer to the problem of human existence.'

ERIC FROMM

Whenever you feel fear, anxiety, worry, anger, stress, jealousy, greed, or other negative states, breathe love into the situation or emotion and detach yourself from it.

For example, if you fear losing your job or a partner, let go of the fear of losing and breathe love into the situation. Accept that whatever happens you will land on your feet. Affirm that you have the job or relationship that will make you happy.

Flip your mind into a loving state. Love is such a powerful force. Not only will you feel better, but the Law Of Attraction will respond accordingly too. Feeling love means you are attracting more love into your life right now.

The power of positivity case study

Steve, 43, a financial consultant, discovered me on Google. He was having trouble sleeping and suffering from daily mood swings. He was thinking very negatively about almost everything and had very low self-belief. He had seen a number of hypnotherapists but none had been able to help him find peace of mind.

After teaching him how to project a more positive energy towards his work, relationships and life in general by using self-hypnosis, Steve began to feel real peace of mind. He says he maintains this more peaceful state by listening to my self-hypnosis CDs on a daily basis.

As a result of thinking positively, he has since started his own business; his relationships have improved and he feels much more relaxed.

TIP 8 – *Protect yourself from negativity*

When you experience negativity from outside influences you can still remain in your own centred space and stay in a place of strength

The golden rule is to not get caught up in other people's ego-driven dramas. Ego-driven behaviour is a need to conquer, impress and dominate and is at odds with someone expressing themselves in a loving, compassionate way. You can remain kind and loving towards them but don't let their behaviour bring you down with them.

Here is a short visualisation that can help you feel protected from any negative outside energy. You can use it to deflect criticism or if others try to impose themselves on you or hold you back in any way.

Never underestimate the power of simple visualisations. When you visualise and focus you are tapping into the powerful creative part of your mind that knows no limitation.

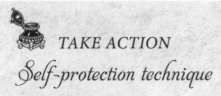

TAKE ACTION
Self-protection technique

- **Close your eyes and take a few slow deep breaths.**

- **Imagine you are surrounded by a white protective light.** Visualise a protective energy field all around your body, as though you have stepped inside a white bubble of pure healing light.

- **When you imagine this light around you, you will feel completely safe and secure.** No negative energy can pass through this protective shield. If anyone criticises you or tries to knock you down, it will bounce off your protective shield and have no effect on you. Only positive thoughts and energy can pass through your protective light.

Anytime you imagine you are inside this white bubble in your everyday life, you will immediately feel protected from outside negativity.

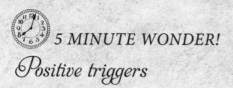

5 MINUTE WONDER!

Positive triggers

A good way to build a positive outlook is to incorporate triggers into your routine that remind you to keep positive. These triggers can become habit forming once you have done them a few times. The triggers could be anything that you feel will be a good daily reminder such as:

- Feeling the water on your head once you have stepped into the shower.
- Taking your seat on the train to work.
- Placing your hands on the car steering wheel each time you drive.

Use these triggers to spend five minutes each day indulging yourself in positive affirmations.

- I look for the positive in every situation.
- I release any negative thoughts or feelings.
- I feel positive and optimistic.
- I deserve the very best life has to offer.

This will help you to programme your mind to be more positive. If you went to the gym every day you would build a toned and fit body. Similarly, when you use these techniques every day you build a very positive mindset.

SUMMARY

- According to the Law of Attraction, whatever you focus on will become a reality so you need to generate as many positive thoughts and feelings as possible.

- Sometimes all you need to do is change your perspective – you need constantly to see the world through positive eyes.

- Taking on new challenges gives you a sense of empowerment and will inspire you to achieve many more goals.

- To help you succeed with any challenge you take on, visualise it beforehand in a 100 per cent positive light.

- When you notice a negative thought, flip it. Change it immediately into something more positive that makes you feel good.

- Note how you are feeling – if you're feeling bad then look at the thoughts behind your feelings and CHANGE them.

- Be selective about what you read and watch.

- Gratitude is a very good way to flip out of negative thinking and feel more positive.

- Whenever you feel negative emotional states, breathe love into the situation or emotion and detach yourself from it.

- Protect yourself from negativity using the *self-protection technique* on page 89.

- Incorporate triggers into your daily routine that remind you to keep positive.

Energy

8

Enhance the Results

'I am convinced that there are universal currents of
Divine Thought vibrating the ether everywhere and
that any who can feel these vibrations is inspired.'

RICHARD WAGNER

Now that we've awakened you to the power of *The Answer* and
you are glowing with positivity, it's time to enhance the results.
There are six techniques I'm going to show you.

In this chapter you will:

- Discover how laughter, healthy food, exercise and loving thoughts
  all assist the process.
- Increase your magnetic power.
- Become more heart-centred and full of love.
- Understand the importance of being present.
- Get creative with your imagination.
- Realise the power of music and the lunar calendar.

1. Good vibrations

The first technique is to raise your energy and vibrational field (easier than it sounds).

Quantum physics maintains that everything in the Universe is a mass of molecules and atoms vibrating at certain frequencies. The chair or bed you might be sitting or lying on now is made up of atoms and molecules that are vibrating so fast that they make the chair or bed appear solid.

We are communicating with the world around us through our subtle energy fields all the time.

When you consistently project clear, positive goals out into the Universe, you will only attract good into your life. You won't connect with people or events of a low energy vibration.

By raising your vibration you will improve the quality of your life in so many ways. Chance meetings and great opportunities will come your way. Things will flow into your life easily. Serendipitous events will occur regularly.

In short, you will easily attract good things and align yourself with opportunity when you build a positive energy field through the techniques in *The Answer*.

A lifestyle choice

Our vibrational energy field is determined by our thoughts, feelings and lifestyle.

If you eat healthily, exercise often, sleep well, laugh a lot and are full of positive thoughts and ideas, your vibrational energy will be high.

Meditation and self-hypnosis will help you raise your vibration as by going inside and calming your mind and body you stop burning energy. In a deep state of relaxation your energy will begin to replenish itself and your vibration will grow stronger.

I believe that when your vibration is high you can manifest the things you want more quickly and easily. Because your energy field is strong and clear, the thoughts and feelings you emit will be stronger and clearer. You will become healthier and be less susceptible to illness and disease.

You will also become more intuitive. People will be drawn to you without realising why.

> *'When your energy is strong you will find your powers of attracting are more magnetic.'*

Conversely, too much alcohol, smoking, drug taking (both medicinal and recreational), lack of sleep and negative thoughts and feelings are all things that will lower your vibration and create a dense, sluggish energy field around you. This will make it harder for you to attract what you want and you will struggle your way through life.

If you follow these tips below at least 80 per cent of the time you will raise your energy and vibrational field and become more of a magnet for what you desire.

TAKE ACTION

How to raise your vibration

1. **Meditate or use self-hypnosis** regularly – by switching off your intellectual mind and connecting with positive thoughts and feelings you will allow your cells to recharge and feel more relaxed and energised.

2. **Exercise** regularly – this will increase your metabolism and help you to feel more energetic.

3. **Laugh, smile and be happy!**

4. **Be careful what you absorb**. Avoid reading newspapers, trashy magazines or watching too much TV, especially negative, fear-based programmes.

5. **Eat healthily** – stick to three main meals a day and only eat fruit and vegetables in-between meals.

6. **Drink lots of mineral or filtered water** each day and avoid sugary drinks like Coke or soda.

7. **Avoid too much alcohol and don't smoke or take any kind of drug** unless instructed by a doctor or physician. These three things will lower your vibrational energy so use sparingly.

8. **Some say avoiding meat** is a good way to raise your energy. I am a vegetarian for this reason but I understand this is a personal choice and I don't want to preach.

9. **Protect your positive energy**. Once your energy field is strong, others might gravitate towards you and you may need to work on protecting yourself. Imagine a strong white light around you that no negative energy can penetrate (see page 89). You can still be kind and compassionate with people but you need to retain your own strength and good energy.

2. Love, Love, Love

'Let your love be like the misty rains, coming softly, but flooding the river.'

MALAGASY PROVERB

Whenever you meet one of the special rare human beings who are very loving but also strong, they have an amazing magnetism.

Work on building a powerful inner strength and giving your love freely through actions of kindness and compassion.

Love is all that matters in this world so why not let it flow through your life?

Heart-centred goals

Infusing your goals with love will give them a powerful resonance and a purity of intention.

My aim with *The Answer* is to teach you how to use the Law of Attraction from a very heart-centred place so that your projections have a purity to them.

By projecting from a loving, harmonious place while in a deep state of relaxation you will be projecting with a pure, high vibrational energy. You will manifest things easily and effortlessly.

*'Beauty is not in the face;
beauty is a light in the heart.'*

KAHLIL GIBRAN

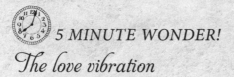

5 MINUTE WONDER!

The love vibration

Use this technique anytime you're around people – when you walk down the street, or meet people for the first time or with people you know. It will help you to start to develop more love in your life and will raise your vibration.

Wherever you go make a habit of projecting a positive feeling of love to everyone you pass by. Imagine a strong feeling of love coming from your heart and reaching their heart, and silently focus on the word 'love'. When you do this, avoid judgement or discrimination.

Practise this technique with anyone and everyone: family, friends, acquaintances and strangers.

'Spread love into every goal
you focus on and express love
in everything you do.'

TAKE ACTION

Infusing your goals with love technique

- **Close your eyes and imagine someone you love dearly**, preferably unconditionally. It can be a child, parent, a relative or a close friend.

- **Focus on how much you love this person**, think of all their positive traits and connect with a warm loving feeling towards them. Take a few minutes to really connect with this strongly.

- **Imagine your heart opening and a light shining out** from its centre. Put your feelings into this and allow this feeling of love to grow stronger all the time.

- **Now allow your mind to go blank** for a few minutes but hold on to the feeling of love. Let the feeling grow stronger all the time.

- **When you are ready focus on one of your goals** and project the feeling of love towards it. Infuse it with pure unconditional love. Imagine the light from your heart engulfing every aspect of your goal.

- **Continue to feel the love and let go of any conscious thought**. Allow yourself to relax deeply and let your feelings grow stronger all the time.

- **Do this for as long as you wish** and then when you are ready to finish open your eyes and become wide awake.

This technique is one you can use little and often. Ten minutes at a time once or twice a day would be ideal but if you want to do it more that's fine.

'To give and not expect return, that is what lies at the heart of love.'

OSCAR WILDE

Love

3. Be present

> *'With the past, I have nothing to do;*
> *nor with the future. I live now.'*

RALPH WALDO EMERSON

To raise your vibration higher still it is important to practise being present and living your life in the here and now.

So often our minds drift into the future or back into the past. Worrying about a future event achieves nothing but anxiety.

Think of all the things you worried about last week – most of the things you feared won't have actually happened. Worrying was a complete waste of energy. In chapter 15 I go into detail about how to let go of fear and worries. Conserve and build your energy by remaining present as much as possible

> *'The living moment is everything.'*

D.H. LAWRENCE

Relax and connect to the moment. . .

So much of our day is about doing and so little is about just being. Whether you're a busy mother of four or a city high flyer it only takes a few minutes to reconnect to the present moment.

Taking time out to relax is a great way to do this. When you go into a state of mental and physical relaxation, your brainwaves will slow down from the beta to alpha state and beyond, allowing mind and body to recharge and rejuvenate.

You'll feel refreshed afterwards even if you only relax for a few minutes. The technique below is ideal for lunch breaks but can be used anytime you need a boost.

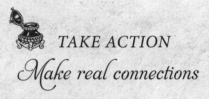

TAKE ACTION
Make real connections

- When you talk to people really be there with them.

- Make real eye contact and connect with them, whoever they are.

- Stay in the moment. This will help you to feel more present and live your life in the moment.

A walk with a difference

Walking in nature is another great way to feel present and connected.

Whenever you have the opportunity, go outside and walk more in nature. As you do look up at the sky and imagine your goals and dreams out there in the Universe.

Imagine that a higher power is supercharging them and turning them into a reality. Lie on the ground and look up at the sky and imagine your dream as a reality now. See the infinite sky and know there are amazing possibilities everywhere and that you have so much potential. The Universe is listening and hearing everything that you are projecting out there.

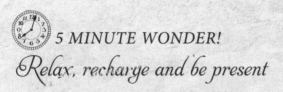

5 MINUTE WONDER!
Relax, recharge and be present

This short relaxation exercise will help you to:

- Become more present.
- Recharge your energy.
- Be more effective for the rest of your day.

1. **Take time out**. Find a quiet place in your break time where you won't be disturbed and practise the following technique.

2. **Get comfortable**. Sit or lie comfortably. If you are sitting on a chair, sit upright with your feet flat on the floor and your hands flat on your thighs.

3. **Breathe**. Close your eyes and begin to breathe very slowly and deeply in through your nose and out through

your mouth. Make each circular breath long and deep, and continue this relaxing rhythm. Breathe away any tension in your body with every out breath and feel yourself connecting to the present moment. Be aware as each second passes.

4. **Clear your mind**. The aim is to clear away any thoughts so your mind becomes still and centred. This can be a challenge if you have had a busy day or there is noise around you. If that is the case, affirm to yourself that any outside noise will fade into the background and will help you to relax even more. Remember when you state this as a fact your unconscious mind will accept it. Don't worry if you get the odd unwanted thought. Just centre your mind again and allow the thought to drift away. Focus on your slow deep breathing and feel a strong connection to the present moment.

5. **Be present**. Stay in this relaxed state for five, ten or even twenty minutes and then allow yourself to come back to full waking consciousness. Be still, centred and very present.

4. Visualising – with your senses

Using visual imagery as well as words when in a hypnotic state is a very powerful way of absorbing beliefs into your unconscious mind.

When visualising, use all your senses. For instance, if you've always dreamt of living by the sea:

See yourself in the kitchen of your dream house. Notice the aromas of the pots of herbs on the shelf. Hear the sound of the sea outside.

Or if you're anxious about a upcoming meeting or event·

See the shape and size of the room. Notice the colours of the walls and carpet. Feel your clothes against your skin. Hear the sound of your voice expressing yourself confidently and clearly.

- Always see yourself in a completely positive light.
- Run the images through your mind using as much detail as possible.
- Use as many of your senses as you can.

'Using visual imagery as well as words when in a hypnotic state is a very powerful way of absorbing beliefs into your unconscious mind.'

Your unconscious mind cannot differentiate between what is real and imagined. So the more often you imagine a future situation in a positive light, when it actually happens in reality it will believe that you have been there before.

You will feel as composed and in control as you were when you visualised it during the 'mental rehearsal'.

5. The power of music

Music has an incredible power to make us feel a whole range of emotions. Think of a song that makes you feel really happy and inspired and another song that makes you feel really sad.

That's because not only do different sounds and tones have an impact on our mood, but the memories and feelings we associate with particular songs give them a meaning for us; either one that is positive or one that is negative.

Follow the simple instructions opposite to supercharge the Law of Attraction using the power of music.

This technique works wonderfully because you can listen to your song or songs whenever you want to generate these feelings again. You can even have different pieces of music for different desired feelings and make a playlist that you can listen to whenever you like.

No matter what situation you are in, you can change your emotional state easily by using the power of music.

5 MINUTE WONDER!

The power of music exercise

1. **Decide what you want to achieve** or attract. For example, a new job.

2. **Choose an appropriate desired feeling**, according to what you want to achieve. Do you want to feel confident? Enthusiastic? Happy and full of life? Or perhaps relaxed and centred?

3. **Choose a piece of music** that makes you feel really positive and one that matches your desired outcome and feeling. So if you want to feel confident then an upbeat piece of music may be most suitable, whereas if you want to feel calm and centred, a softer and slower piece of music may suit you better. If it's a song with lyrics then make sure the lyrics are positive.

4. **Go somewhere quiet** where you won't be disturbed and find a relaxing, comfortable position, either sitting or lying down and then close your eyes.

5. **Play your chosen piece of music on repeat**, preferably through headphones. Remember times in your past

when you felt this confident, calm or joyful (or whatever feeling you are focusing on.)

6. **Become completely absorbed in the music and imagine those good feelings** flowing through every part of you. If it helps, you can imagine the positive feelings as a colour. Imagine that colour flowing around your body and becoming brighter as the good feelings intensify.

7. **When you're feeling really good, start to visualise** your desired outcome as a movie. For example, if you want a new job then visualise seeing yourself at work in your new job looking happy and content. How do you look? What are you doing? Who's around you? Make this film as clear as you can, with lots of detail. The colours should be vivid and bright.

8. **Imagine stepping into that movie**, so that instead of seeing yourself you are completely involved in it and experiencing what's going on as though it's really happening to you now. Spend at least five minutes doing this and then open your eyes when you feel ready to continue with the rest of your day.

6. Full moons and special days

Using the Law of Attraction to project your goals on special dates in the lunar calendar can have an added impact. It is said that universal energy has increased strength at full moons, eclipses, equinoxes and at the summer and winter solstices.

Case study on the power of a full moon

A couple of years ago I had a large space at my office to rent. It was at the height of the recession and we had only had one viewing in 18 months. It seemed like an impossible task to get the space rented which was frustrating as we still had to pay full rates and other costs on the space.

One night at a full moon I sat in my garden projecting a goal of getting the ideal company to rent the space. I spent an hour gazing up at the beautiful full moon and imagining an honourable company with nice people working in our office space. I went into detail and got into a deep inner space and put strong feelings into my projections.

The very next morning we received a call from a woman who wanted to rent our office space. She had a great company and the space and location worked for her. She became our perfect tenant. Her business was even in the same self-help/healing field as ours. Twelve hours after I used the Law Of Attraction to manifest a goal it happened just as I had imagined. Two years on she is still renting the space and our businesses work in perfect harmony.

SUMMARY

- By raising your vibration you will improve the quality of your life in so many ways.

- When your energy is strong you will find your powers of attracting are more magnetic.

- You will easily attract good things and align yourself with opportunity when you build a positive energy field through the techniques in *The Answer*.

- If you eat healthily, exercise often, sleep well, laugh a lot and are full of positive thoughts and ideas, your vibrational energy will be high.

- Self-hypnosis and meditation will help you raise your vibration.

- Spread love into every goal you focus on and express love in everything you do.

- Practise being present and living your life in the here and now.

- Walking in nature is another great way to feel present and connected.

- When visualising your goals use all your senses.

- You can change your emotional state by using the power of music.

- Project your goals on special dates in the lunar calendar to have an added impact.

'If you want to find the secrets of the Universe, think in terms of energy, frequency and vibration.'

NIKOLA TESLA

Part Two

Compassion

9

Love and Relationships

'The good man is the friend of all living things.'

MAHATMA GANDHI

You can use *The Answer* to attract more love and harmony into your relationships.

In essence, this is very simple.

You simply project love to others.

When you make this a habit you will attract back more of the same and your relationships will improve.

Relationship problems are often caused by differing views or because other people don't always live up to our expectations and we don't always live up to theirs.

'Cherish your human connections:
your relationships with friends and family.'

JOSEPH BRODSKY

Obviously communication is an important way to resolve disputes and differences of opinion. Hoping the other person will change or suddenly see things your way is unlikely unless you communicate.

But the best way to solve a relationship problem is to project love onto the situation and towards that person.

This can sometimes be a challenge, especially if you feel particularly wronged by someone but projecting love is ultimately going to help you to grow and move on.

My *harmonious relationships technique* (see the box below) will help you improve your relationships. It will also help you to feel more love and compassion. As always, practise it regularly to get the best results.

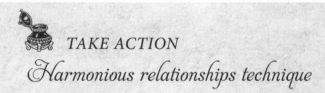

TAKE ACTION
Harmonious relationships technique

Use this technique to improve your relationships and develop more love and compassion for others. Read the following script through a few times before you practise it.

- **Take yourself off to a quiet room** where there are no distractions.

- **Close your eyes and focus your attention on your breathing**. Begin breathing slowly and deeply until you feel relaxed and centred.

- **Become aware of your heart, and connect with a very loving feeling**. Think of someone you love dearly and imagine your heart is filled with pure white light, a white light that resonates with unconditional love.

- **Feel this white light of love growing in your heart**. Imagine the white light expanding out from your heart so that it begins to fill your whole body. Feel a strong sense of love and compassion for all things.

- **Now imagine the white light expanding**, filling your entire body and spreading out into your aura and further still. Make this deep feeling of love and compassion in your heart grow stronger and stronger and imagine that the white light projects out and away from your body in every direction.

- **Visualise your white light of unconditional love reaching out** now and engulfing others. It can be to people you know or to individuals who you want to improve relations with. Or it can be general.

- **Imagine the white light streaming from your heart embracing others**, and feel a strong feeling of love for these people. And feel a deep compassion for their struggles and troubles, seeing their faults and weaknesses as manifestations of difficulties in their life.

- **Connect with a powerful feeling of love and compassion** for others while you are in this deeply relaxed state.

- **At this point, you can also create some affirmations** to compound this feeling of love and compassion. State your affirmations as a reality now in the present tense. Here are some examples, but please adapt and add your own to suit your needs:

  I love to develop positive relationships with people.
  I am full of forgiveness and love.
  I give and receive love easily.

- When you state your affirmations, draw the words inside you and really **believe they are a reality**. Put positive feelings of love into each phrase and totally believe in what you are affirming. The more you believe in the phrases, the stronger they will become.

- **Practise this technique a few times** and repeat the affirmations regularly to get the best results.

- **When you are ready to finish**, allow you mind to clear and count slowly upwards from one to ten, and open your eyes and come back to full waking consciousness. 1… 2… 3… 4… 5… 6… 7… 8… 9…10…Wide awake and full of love!

*'An eye for an eye makes
the whole world blind.'*

MAHATMA GANDHI

Attract more love into your life

Now you're worked on improving your relationships, you might want to try the *pure love meditation* on the next page.

Perhaps you want to attract a loving soul mate into your life. Or perhaps you're feeling a bit lonely and unloved.

Whatever the case, the *pure love meditation* is a powerful way to attract more love into your life as you are working with very pure intentions. The meditation will help you connect with a strong feeling of heart energy and will raise your vibration (see page 194).

'Connect with a powerful feeling of love and compassion for others while you are in a deeply relaxed state.'

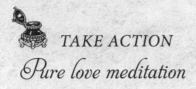

TAKE ACTION

Pure love meditation

Use this meditation to attract more love into your life. Read this script through a few times before you practise it.

1. **Close your eyes and breathe** slowly and deeply.

2. **Relax your mind and body** and allow yourself to let go of all thought. Breathe in through your nose and out through your mouth and relax deeper with every breath. Take a few minutes to get very centred.

3. **Think of someone you love deeply**, more than anyone. Think only of the love you have for this person and feel that love in your heart and let it grow.

4. **Imagine your heart glowing with a pure white light**, a loving white light. Be aware that this is a very pure energy – pure unconditional love – the kind of love a mother feels for her baby. Now imagine the white light expanding out from your heart so that it begins to fill your whole body and energy field.

5. **Let go and go down another level**, deeper and deeper and imagine this white light expanding further so that it projects out and away from you in every direction.

6. **Feel the love growing stronger and stronger** and the white light growing ever brighter as it reaches further and further. Relax into this and really engage your feelings. Feel the pure vibration grow stronger.

*'A loving heart is the beginning
of all knowledge.'*

THOMAS CARLYLE

7. **Imagine your white light reaching out** now and engulfing others. People you know. And feel a deep compassion for their struggles and troubles. Project unconditional love to them.

8. **Continue to expand your love and compassion** further so it reaches out to all things, to all of humanity, to all animals, to the Earth and out into the Universe and beyond. Connect with a feeling of pure love and compassion, of knowledge and personal power. Feel your energy grow stronger all the time. Continue to lose yourself in this powerful projection and spend as long as you wish projecting the love.

9. **When you feel ready to come back** just imagine roots coming out of the bottom of your feet. See these roots go down into the heart of the Earth where there is a pink pool of energy – the energy of Mother Earth – which has unconditional love and compassion for you. Imagine your roots going deep into the Earth, connecting with this energy. Draw this pink light up into your body, fill your heart with this unconditional love and compassion. Allow this energy to expand and permeate though out your body and into every cell of your being. Feel warm, safe and grounded now and back in the present moment.

You can do this projection for as long or short a time as you wish.

'*Affection is responsible for nine-tenths of whatever solid and durable happiness there is in our lives.*'

C.S. LEWIS

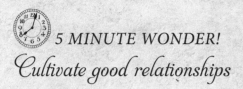

5 MINUTE WONDER!

Cultivate good relationships

Open your heart and project positive feelings to others. People respond well to kindness and compliments and you will often see your generosity reflected back to you.

Spend five minutes daily focusing on your relationships with other people, and think about their positive points and what you like about them. Even very negative people usually have some redeeming features so try to look for the good in people. Then when the time is right express those positive thoughts and feelings to them with honesty and sincerity.

Being generous with your words costs nothing, so make it a habit. Practise the art of being kind and generous with your words every day. A single compliment can change someone's day and make you feel good too. When you do this consistently your relationships will improve as people will reflect your kindness back to you.

'Love is the only force capable of transforming an enemy into friend.'

MARTIN LUTHER KING JR

SUMMARY

- You can use *The Answer* to attract more love and harmony in your relationships.

- The best way to solve a relationship problem is to project love onto the situation and towards that person.

- Connect with a powerful feeling of love and compassion for others while you are in a deeply relaxed state (using the techniques in this chapter).

- To improve your relationships and develop more compassion use my *harmonious relationships* technique.

- To attract more love into your life use my *pure love* meditation.

- Spend five minutes daily focusing on your relationships with other people and think about their positive points and what you like about them.

Vitality

10

Good Health

'It is health that is real wealth
and not pieces of gold and silver.'

MAHATMA GANDHI

A re you tired of feeling sluggish all the time?
Do you often wish you had more energy?

Do you wish you could shift some weight but have a weakness for crisps, chocolate or other fatty foods?

In chapter 8 I talked about how staying fit and healthy is so important for making *The Answer* work for you. On page 96 I gave you tips for keeping your energy and vibration high and these included maintaining a healthy diet and exercising regularly.

Yet in this age of supermarket aisles heaving with tempting foods it can be a struggle to stay off the ice cream. And when you're feeling sluggish, joining a gym or exercise class feels even harder.

In this chapter you will learn how to use self-hypnosis to increase your motivation to:

- Cut cravings for junk food.
- Increase your desire to exercise.

When you are fit and healthy you will also feel happier and more content so read on...

Obese nation: the bigger picture

The results of people eating too much fatty, sugary foods and not doing enough exercise are grimly illustrated by a recent shocking study.

In August 2011 a study by the Mailman School of Public Health at New York's Columbia University revealed that by 2030 half of all Americans will be obese. Currently 32 per cent of all men and 35 per cent of all women are obese. I would imagine Europe will be close behind.

This study states that obesity is fast replacing tobacco as the single most important preventable cause of chronic non-communicable diseases, and will add an extra 7.8 million cases of diabetes, 6.8 million cases of heart disease and stroke, and 539,000 cases of cancer in the US within the next two decades.

'He who has health,
has hope; and he who has hope,
has everything.'

THOMAS CARLYLE

Health starts in the mind

The bottom line is you can take steps towards controlling your health. It is your choice.

You will need to shop wisely, retain some self-discipline and move your body regularly but that is a small price to pay compared to feeling overweight, tired and lazy and worrying about heart disease, diabetes and other illnesses.

Health and fitness really does start in your mind.

By thinking like a fit and healthy person you will become one. You can maintain a fit healthy body and live a long active life if you wish. Here's how.

Eat healthily and exercise regularly

There is nothing more complicated about it than that!

Most weight loss and health programmes only teach you to eat healthily and exercise on a conscious level. The only way to guarantee lasting commitment to any new pattern of behaviour is to re-programme your mind, and not just the part of the mind that deals with your conscious self.

This is where self-hypnosis steps in.

To succeed in creating a fit healthy body in the long term you need to work at a deeper, unconscious level. Better still, by programming your unconscious mind, becoming fit and healthy doesn't have to be a struggle anymore.

If you want to focus on this area in more depth my book *Lose Weight Now* and my hypnosis audio title *Exercise and Fitness Motivation* can help. For now here is a self-hypnosis exercise you can use.

'To build your fitness levels in the long term, you must create a mindset that loves being active and healthy.'

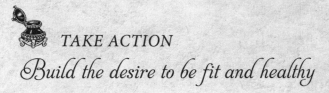

TAKE ACTION
Build the desire to be fit and healthy

This exercise will help you build a powerful desire to become fit and healthy or lose weight (if that's what you need to do).

- **Close your eyes and breathe slowly and deeply**, in through your nose and out through your mouth in a circular breathing motion.

- **Breathe away any tension in your body** with every slow out-breath and allow yourself to relax more and more.

- **Continue this breathing pattern** a dozen times or more, and clear away any unwanted thoughts so that your mind becomes still and quiet. Simply focus on the stillness of the moment.

- **Now visualise yourself looking slim, fit, and healthy**. See yourself looking so good and feeling so attractive and confident.

- **Imagine that you have created a new lifestyle** where you are super strict with what you eat and where you exercise daily. . . and YOU LOVE IT!

- **Imagine doing all the things that keep you fit** such as doing lots of different exercises. Maybe you have joined a tennis club or a dance class. See yourself immersed in this wonderful healthy lifestyle where you eat super healthily and banish all junk food and alcohol completely. Most importantly see yourself enjoying the rewards of having a healthy body.

- **Use all of your senses to make it real**. Feel the clothes against your skin over your slim figure. Run your hands down your slim, toned physique and praise yourself. Connect with a strong feeling of love for yourself. Open your heart and feel good as you do this. Amplify the positive feelings and make the image big, bright, and clear.

- **Now accept on every level that this is what you deserve**. Using your feelings here is key. Really feel, on a deep level, that you love looking so slim, healthy and attractive. Take a moment to resonate with these positive feelings. When you do this, these feelings and images will sink into your unconscious mind and become a part of your inner reality. Your unconscious mind will see this positive image of yourself and accept it as real.

- **When you are ready to finish**, allow you mind to clear by slowly counting up to ten. Open your eyes, and come back to full waking consciousness. When you reach ten, every part of you will be back in the here and now.

Practise this technique often, especially when your health is an issue.

A change for life

Being fit and healthy will improve your life in so many ways. It will raise your energy and vibration and help you achieve other goals more easily. In general you will feel much happier and more content in yourself and will your self-confidence will improve.

To build your fitness levels in the long term, you must create a mindset that loves being active and healthy. Work on your health goals one at a time. So many people initially build a strong resolve to get fit, only to give up after three months and drift back to their old, unhealthy ways.

*'To keep the body in good health is a duty...
otherwise we shall not be able to keep our mind
strong and clear.'*

BUDDHA

Think of the fable of the tortoise and the hare, in which the slow but steady pace of the tortoise brings success. Use this story as a metaphor for your own long-term success. Work on your fitness and health gradually by doing a little each day, building up to a level that feels good for you.

SUMMARY

- Good health and fitness are important for making *The Answer* work for you.

- When you are fit and healthy you will also feel happier and more content.

- By thinking like a fit and healthy person you will become one.

- To build your fitness levels in the long term, you must create a mindset that loves being active and healthy. You need to work at a deeper, unconscious level through self-hypnosis.

- To help generate a powerful desire to become fit and healthy or lose weight try the exercise on page 134.

- Work on your fitness and health gradually by doing a little each day, building up to a level that feels good for you.

Abundance

11

Wealth

'All the breaks you need in life wait within your imagination, imagination is the workshop of your mind, capable of turning mind energy into accomplishment and wealth.'

NAPOLEON HILL

Over the course of *The Answer*, I have shown you how to supercharge your goals and make them happen by using the Law of Attraction combined with self-hypnosis.

Perhaps you have already experimented with goals that aimed for more money using the techniques outlined in *The Answer*.

This chapter focuses on wealth and money in more detail and will help you if you're after the following:

- A higher salary.
- A profitable business.
- A home of your own – or a bigger or a second home.

- A healthy bank balance.
- The car of your dreams.

'Wealth, like happiness, is never attained when sought after directly. It comes as a by-product of providing a useful service.'

HENRY FORD

The key elements for creating wealth

If you want to be wealthy, or at least financially comfortable, you can be. It really is that simple.

The key is to believe that being wealthy is a reality now, as well as following a few basic steps outlined below.

1. **Avoid debt, repay loans and rein in spending** (until you are actually rich). Make sure your income always exceeds your spending. If you are broke, stick to only buying essentials for now until your circumstances change.

'When you surround yourself with wealth and success the Law of Attraction will respond to you.'

2. **Let go of any worry or stress about financial matters**. Avoid talking about money in a negative way, even if you don't have much. Accept and believe that abundance will soon come to you.

3. **Feel positive about money** and start to make lots of plans to make more. There are always opportunities to make money even in economic recessions.

4. **Now focus on what you actually want**. If you want to become wealthy and own a thriving business and huge houses then believe this is going to be your reality. If you just want a little more, then that is also fine, just be clear about what you actually want.

5. **Write down your financial goals** that you want to achieve and include a time frame. For example, 'Goals for November 2012' could be:

   - I own a one million pound house.
   - I run my own thriving business.
   - I make lots of money working ten hours a week from home.

6. **Read your goals every day and recite the following affirmations** on a daily basis.

   - I am wealthy and abundant.
   - I am always in the right place at the right time.
   - Abundance flows freely and naturally to me.
   - All of my needs are constantly met.

These affirmations are very powerful and when you affirm them regularly you will build up a strong energy. When you recite the affirmations believe they are a reality NOW. Belief is very powerful and something all successful people have in abundance. Get into the habit of silently affirming these phrases when you awaken, when you shower, when you are driving or anytime throughout the day when you have some dead time.

7. **Be proactive**. Once you have created the belief you then need to be proactive, put yourself in the marketplace where you can attract more money into your life. If you are already in a full-time job, maybe start a little sideline that has big potential.

'I think when you spread the wealth around it's good for everybody.'

BARACK OBAMA

My story

I once lived in a drab flat at the top of a council tower block in a poor area of South London and made a living driving a mini cab around the West End of London in the evening.

Even though I was struggling and faced many challenging situations I always had the belief that my circumstances would change one day. For me it was through reading books like this and realising that I held the power inside me to change my circumstances.

When I discovered and began using the Law of Attraction combined with self-hypnosis, I became empowered for the first time and my life soon changed beyond recognition.

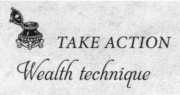

TAKE ACTION

Wealth technique

Use this technique to develop the strong inner belief needed to attract wealth. When you believe this on a deep unconscious level you are sending out a powerful statement of intent. With this type of unconscious programming you will find doors will open for you and you will attract just what you need to become more wealthy and abundant into your life.

- **Close your eyes and imagine** yourself living a truly wealthy life with everything you desire.

- **See your dream home, job, holidays and lifestyle** and imagine it is a reality NOW. Feel your skin touching the comfortable sofa in your luxury home. Imagine your hands on the steering wheel of your dream car. Whatever you desire imagine it happening now.

- **Now project all these goals out into the Universe** with an open heart and ask that they manifest for the highest good of all concerned. Accept on every level that you deserve the best life has to offer and that everything will come easily to you.

- **Believe you are wealthy NOW**, even if your bank statement says otherwise. Always carry plenty of cash with you, don't leave it all in the bank. Go for tea at the Dorchester or any nice hotel. Window-shop in Harrods and if you can, hang out with people who are rich, ambitious and motivated. When you surround yourself with wealth and success the Law Of Attraction will respond to you.

- **Train yourself to see opportunities around you** and see the positive in situations. Taking full responsibility for your life can be difficult at times but ultimately this is the key to real self-empowerment. This is how you turn the tide and start attracting wealth. You will start to create your life and master your destiny rather than being a victim of circumstance.

- **Most importantly you must believe that you absolutely deserve to be abundant and successful.**

'The greatest danger for most of us is not that our aim is too high and we miss it, but that it is too low and we reach it.'

MICHELANGELO

'Wealth is well known to be a great comforter.'

PLATO

Case study - lottery win

I have known June for 25 years as she has been married to my father for that time. June had quite a tough upbringing but has always been a very positive, glass half full type of person. She recently told me that when she was young she always had a very strong belief that she would one day win a lot of money in a lottery.

So strong was her belief that she would often tell people this. She says that it felt like an absolute certainty but she didn't know why. From deep within her unconscious mind she could sense that it was part of her destiny.

In the mid 1980s she was working and living in Canada when she entered the Saturday lottery as she often did. She memorised her seven random numbers and as she drove home she heard the winning numbers being read out on her car radio. At that point she recognised the numbers as being the ones on her ticket. On getting home she checked her ticket and they matched the numbers she had heard on the radio.

As there was no internet available back then she had to wait until a TV station broadcast the winning numbers later that evening. This confirmed she had all seven numbers in the Canadian lottery and had won the equivalent of well over £1,000,000 in today's money.

June says that at the time she didn't feel shocked because she always 'knew' this was going to happen so she was well prepared for it. Many lottery winners have said the same – that they always 'knew' they were going to win. When she rang her sister in the UK to tell her she had some news the first thing her sister said was: 'Have you won the lottery?' She really wasn't joking as June had told her so many times it was going to happen. Her belief was so strong that she had created a very powerful energy around winning the lottery. When your belief is that strong the Universe will always deliver!

SUMMARY

- Avoid debt, repay loans and rein in spending.

- Let go of any worry or stress about financial matters.

- Feel positive about money and start to make lots of plans to make more.

- Focus on what you actually want and write down your financial goals.

- Read or recite your goals and affirmations every day.

- Be proactive – put yourself in the marketplace.

- Use the *wealth technique* on page 143 to develop the strong inner belief needed to attract wealth.

Success

12
Career

'Belief in oneself is one of the most important bricks in building any successful venture.'

LYDIA M. CHILD

Being successful in career and money terms can mean different things to different people. Perhaps a steady job with regular income is enough to make you feel secure and happy. Or perhaps you are someone who needs big goals and challenges to thrive.

- Think about what you really want from your career.
- Be clear about what you want to achieve, both financially and in your work.
- Write down the things you want to achieve in your work life and the financial security it entails.

Remember to write your goals and affirmations in the present tense as though they are a reality now. By stating your career goal as a present tense reality the Universe will respond accordingly and opportunity will come your way.

> *'Success is simple. Do what's right, the right way, at the right time.'*
>
> ARNOLD H. GLASOW

Don't put a limit on what you want to achieve even if you're faced with obstacles.

Once you've written down what you want to achieve, the following visualisation on page 152 will help you use *The Answer* to project your career goal.

> *'Always bear in mind that your own resolution to succeed is more important than any other.'*
>
> ABRAHAM LINCOLN

*'See yourself clearly in your
ideal work situation and imagine
it is a reality now.'*

The Answer

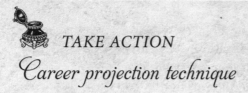

TAKE ACTION
Career projection technique

Use this technique for as long as it takes you to land your dream job or to create a successful business. I recommend you work on this goal continuously even when things start to work out. You may need to adapt it from time to time as you reach your goals and targets but it is one I suggest you continue with and refresh as your career develops. Everything I have achieved in my career has materialised and become a reality because I used this technique.

- **Close your eyes and begin to breathe very slowly and deeply**, in through your nose and out through your mouth. At the top of your breath hold for three seconds, and then count to five on every out-breath. As you breathe out imagine you are breathing away any nervous tension left in your body.

- **Allow your mind to become clear and continue to relax**. Let every muscle in your body become loose and relaxed. Take time to allow yourself to drift into a deeply relaxed and centred space.

- **Imagine you now have the ideal job or career** that you want along with all the financial security that it brings. Imagine your lifestyle clearly.

- **Make your visualisation detailed and colourful**. See yourself clearly in your ideal work situation and imagine it is a reality now. Allow yourself to feel very secure and see yourself coping with any pressure with a new inner strength and calm.

- **Now imagine sending this goal out into the Universe with love**. Imagine you are there now in the career you have always dreamed of. See it in colourful detail and use all your senses.

- **At this point you can also state one or more affirmations** if you wish. Say them over and over like a mantra with total belief and feeling. Here are some examples but use your own affirmations so they relate specifically to your own goal:

I have a secure job with a great salary.
I have my own successful _____ business.
I love and excel in my job.
Opportunities come easily to me.

- **Focus on your goal and affirmations** for as long as you wish. Any time you get a negative thought just allow it to drift away and continue to project positively.

- **When you have finished**, open your eyes and become wide awake.

A note on work stress

If you suffer from work stress, the important thing to do is make changes. If changing jobs is not an option look at what you can do to improve things.

If your workload is excessive, prioritise the most important work. Delegate if you can.

If you work long hours, try at least to get some rest and relaxation.

A break at lunchtime or a short self-hypnosis session (see page 60) can help you relax and recharge to make you more effective for the rest of the day.

'Many of life's failures are people who did not realise how close they were to success when they gave up.'

THOMAS EDISON

SUMMARY

- Write down the things you want to achieve in your work life and the financial security it entails.

- Remember to write your goals and affirmations in the present tense.

- Don't put a limit on what you want to achieve even if you're faced with obstacles.

- Use the *career projection technique* on page 152 for as long as it takes you to land your dream job or to create a successful business.

- If you suffer from work stress, make whatever changes you can. At your break at lunchtime a short self-hypnosis session (see page 60) can help you relax and recharge.

Harmony

13

Home Environment

'Love begins at home, and it is not how much we
do. . . but how much love we put in that action.'

MOTHER TERESA

When using the Law of Attraction and the techniques in *The Answer* it is important to have a clutter-free, calming home environment.

If your house is cluttered the energy will be sluggish, which is not ideal for manifesting.

Your living space needs to be congruent with your Law Of Attraction goals and aims.

It is important to create a home environment that is calming and free of clutter and that feels fresh and alive.

When you walk into a house that is clutter-free and clean, it makes you feel good. Likewise when you never move or clean anything the energy tends to feel dense and cold.

You can actually feel the energy in rooms on an unconscious level so it is important for your mental and emotional well-being that your home makes you feel good and positive.

Tips on de-cluttering

The first step is to clear out clutter and junk and make sure your house is clean.

Create a feeling of space by sparsely furnishing the rooms so they appear larger and lighter.

Don't allow furniture to block windows or doorways and store as much as you can in cupboards. The key is to not get attached to inanimate objects.

Adding a few small plants will help your home feel more alive.

Then try the *visualising a positive and happy home exercise.*

'It is important to create a home environment that is calming and free of clutter and that feels fresh and alive.'

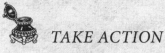

TAKE ACTION

Visualising a positive and happy home

This technique will help you create a harmonious, positive home environment. It will also help improve your relationships with those living in your home.

- **Close your eyes and begin breathing slowly and deeply** – in through your nose and out through your mouth – in a circular breathing motion.

- **Breathe away any tension left in your body** with every slow out-breath, and allow your mind to become still and quiet.

- **In this stillness, imagine a very happy, positive home environment** and see a white protective light all around your house. Feel that your home is safe and protected by this energy at all times.

- **Imagine this white light permeating the space in every room** in the house. See the white light cleansing and healing every area of your home and imagine that everything in your home is harmonious and in balance.

- **Visualise yourself in your home happy and content**. Your relationship with everyone around you is loving and harmonious and there is so much love in your life. Hold this picture for while and make it big, bright and clear. Really feel it is a reality now. Affirm to yourself that these feelings will stay with you.

- **Now, in this relaxed and receptive state, you can silently recite the following affirmations**. You can adapt them or add your own too.

  I have a positive and happy home environment.
  I feel creative and inspired at home and in my work.
  I manifest wonderful things in my life.
  I take on new challenges with a positive attitude.

- **When you are ready to finish**, allow your mind to clear for a minute then count slowly upwards from one to ten. Open your eyes when you reach the number eight and at the number ten you will come back to full waking consciousness.

Repeat this daily.

SUMMARY

- When using the Law of Attraction and the techniques in *The Answer* it is important to have a clutter-free, clean and calming home environment.

- Create a feeling of space by sparsely furnishing the rooms so they

- Don't allow furniture to block windows or doorways and store as much as you can in cupboards.

- Adding a few small plants will help your home feel more alive.

- Try the *visualising a positive and happy home exercise* on page 159 to boost the feeling of harmony in your home and to improve your relationships with those you live with.

Peace

14

Stress

'Stress is basically a disconnection from the Earth, a forgetting of the breath. Stress is an ignorant state. It believes that everything is an emergency. Nothing is that important. Just lie down.'

NATALIE GOLDBERG

S tress is so common now that we almost consider it normal. How often do you hear yourself or those around you say:

'I am so busy I just don't have time.'
'I'm so stressed.'
'I can't cope with this pressure.'

Stress happens when we feel out of control or when we have too much to do with too little time. If you have a house, a mortgage, a busy job, children, friends and family, all these things demand our time. There is only so much time to go round. The more full your life is, the more you can feel pressured and stressed.

Stress can be very draining energetically. In terms of getting *The Answer* to work for you, I have emphasised how vital it is to stay positive (see page 79) and keep your energy levels and vibration as high as possible (see page 94).

So this chapter is for anyone who needs a helping hand in coping with stress.

Symptoms of stress

Not getting too stressed is important for your mental and physical well-being.

The mental and physical symptoms of stress include:

- Anxiety
- Panic attacks
- Insomnia
- Fears and terrors
- Depression
- Mental fatigue
- Nervous exhaustion

- Irritability
- Tension in the body
- Sweating
- Cramp
- Stiff muscles
- Neck and backache
- Irritable bowel syndrome

Extreme prolonged stress can lead to premature ageing, hormonal imbalances, high blood pressure, migraines, arthritis, heart problems, weight issues and more.

Everyone has a different stress threshold and some cope with pressure easier than others. We all know that in small amounts stress can be positive – for instance it can help you make a work deadline or stretch you creatively.

But if your stress levels are pushing you over the edge then the following technique will help you to cope with pressure in stressful situations and detach from negative emotions.

'Tension is who you think you should be.
Relaxation is who you are.'

CHINESE PROVERB

TAKE ACTION

Stress reliever and detachment technique

- Breathing deeply is a great way to control stress and stay calm under pressure. Begin by breathing slowly and deeply in through your nose and out through your mouth in a steady circular rhythm. If you can, close your eyes, but this is not essential. Think of nothing but your breathing.

- Continue this slow, rhythmical breathing and, as you inhale, push your stomach out so that you breathe into your stomach, which then expands slightly. Then, as you exhale, your stomach goes in and your chest slightly expands. This is called diaphragmatic breathing. Practise it for a while until it comes naturally.

- Whenever a problem or stressful situation arises, don't immediately react in a negative way. Breathe diaphragmatically so that you draw more oxygen into your body and up to your brain. Stay calm, suspend any knee-jerk reaction and keep your mind clear.

- Imagine you are stepping out of your body and viewing the situation from above. Remain detached from any emotion or judgement and project positive feelings to the situation.

- Take a few more deep breaths and think about how the problem can be resolved. If there is no obvious solution, think of all the things you can do to improve the situation. If nothing comes to mind straightaway, continue to project positive feelings and affirm that your mind will find solutions when the time is right.

'The greatest weapon against stress is our ability to choose one thought over another.'

WILLIAM JAMES

Learning from stress

When stressful situations arise, be proactive and ask yourself: 'What can I learn from this situation?'

There is always a lesson to be learnt from every difficulty we face in life. Sometimes all we need is to change the way we think. Is it your attitude you need to change (see chapter 7 for tips on positive thinking) or do you need to jump ship and go for that new job, house or relationship?

Case study on empowerment

Marie, 40, now an office manager and personal assistant, suffered extreme anxiety, depression and panic attacks following the births of both her children. Despite having loving caring people around her all the time she felt constantly scared and very alone.

Every day, she felt like she was just going through the motions, feeling dead inside. She could only make short trips out of the house to stay in her comfort zone.

A friend who knew of Marie's situation asked her to a show in London. The thought of this initially scared her but she agreed. Arriving an hour too early she browsed the self-help section of a book store, desperate to help herself. She was drawn to a book on self-hypnosis.

She became engrossed in the self-hypnosis techniques and after using them regularly finally began to feel self-worth again. She started by focusing on what I wanted – to feel more confident when mixing with people. It worked and she felt more in control of her life.

Eventually she felt ready to go back to work and focused on the type of job she wanted (one that was in a caring profession that also allowed for personal growth). She gave this specific goal her total focus at the time and often projected this when she was in self-hypnosis.

She regularly searched the local papers but nothing really struck her until one day she came a across a very basic advert giving minimal information about a part-time job. She was very drawn to the advert but she didn't know why as it really gave very little away. She was drawn to it, even though it was for 20 hours a week and she was worried about the child care cost.

She applied for the job and attended an interview. She soon realised the company and the position were everything she had been asking for, even down to finest of details. Much to her delight, she was offered the job. She didn't know it then (although she does now) but she had been using the Law of Attraction combined with self-hypnosis all along. Getting that job has been positively life changing for her.

'Whenever a problem or stressful situation arises, don't immediately react in a negative way.'

SUMMARY

- Stress can be very draining energetically as well as bad for your health. *The Answer* works best with a positive outlook and high energy levels so try to focus on staying positive (see page 79) and raising your energy (see page 96).

- Breathing deeply is a great way to control stress and stay calm under pressure.

- When you feel yourself getting stressed, avoid getting overemotional, take control of your breathing, project positive feelings to the situation and aim to reframe the problem.

- When stressful situations arise, be proactive and ask yourself: 'What can I learn from this situation?'

- If your stress levels are pushing you over the edge try the *stress reliever and detachment technique* (see page 166) will help you to cope more easily.

Trust

15

Fear

'The whole secret of existence is to have no fear.
Never fear what will become of you, depend on
no one. Only the moment you reject all help are
you freed.'

BUDDHA

Most of our worries come from a need to be secure. The world is a chaotic place and it can be hard not to feel the fear at times. We are living in an age of insecurity and upheaval with huge economies teetering on the edge of bankruptcy.

What if I lose my job?
What if I can't pay off my credit card bill?
What if I can't find 'the one' and remain alone?

So many fears are 'what ifs.' Think of all the things you worried about last week or last year. Most of the things you feared won't have actually happened. Worrying was a complete waste of energy

The Answer can help you master your own mind and avoid much of the fear and worry that permeates the world we live in.

Let go of fear

There are also times when something does go wrong which triggers off a wave of fear. Say you have just lost your job or your boyfriend has just broken up with you.

When things are out of your control and you're feeling the fear, do what you can (whether that's job hunting or joining a dating agency), send love to the situation and meditate on a positive outcome using the exercises in *The Answer*. Then let go of it.

Even when a friend or loved one is in distress, do everything you can to help then, send them love and meditate on a positive outcome then let it go.

Use the techniques you learnt in *The Answer* to keep your focus positive and work on new goals. Try not to get bogged down in fear and worry.

'In time we hate that which we often fear.'

WILLIAM SHAKESPEARE

'Courage is resistance to fear,
mastery of fear, not absence of fear.'

MARK TWAIN

Empower yourself

There are other things you can do to empower yourself in general.

- Detach from unwanted, unhelpful fears and negativity (see *releasing fear and worry meditation* on the next page.)
- Eat very healthily.
- Exercise regularly.
- Focus on generating love to yourself and others. Love is the most powerful force in the Universe and will always overcome darkness.
- Watch and read things that help with your empowerment.
- Avoid television, newspapers, trashy magazines and any kind of media promoting fear, greed and negativity and stay in your own place of strength.

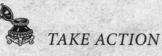

TAKE ACTION

Releasing fear and worry meditation

The following technique will help you calm your mind and alleviate fear, worry and stress.

If you are constantly going over problems in your mind, your thinking and judgement becomes clouded. But when you meditate you allow your mind to rest and recuperate.

You can use this technique for 20 or 30 minutes at a time. You will be amazed at how good you will feel afterwards. You will find that you have a new perspective on problems and can deal with things with greater clarity.

Stop at this point and read the script through a few times until you know what to do and then practise this technique for the next few days. You will find that the more you practise, the deeper into a trance you will go each time, and the better you will get at letting go of fear.

- **Go to a quiet room** where there are no distractions. Light a candle and place it in front of you. Turn off all the lights.

- **Sit comfortably in front of the candle and focus on the flickering flame.** Watch the movement of the flame and begin to breathe very slowly and deeply: in through your nose and out through your mouth. Make each circular breath long and deep, and clear away any thoughts so your mind becomes still and centred. Don't worry if you get the odd unwanted thought. Just centre your mind again and allow the thought to drift away. Focus on your breathing and the stillness of the moment.

- **Keep your eyes on the flame and remain centred and focused. Be in the here and now and accept everything as it is.** Continue with your slow, deep breathing and allow yourself to relax deeply. You can stay in this pleasant state for as long as you like.

- **The first time you practise focus on nothing but clearing your mind and staying centred.** This alone is enough to completely de-stress your mind. Once you have practised this technique a few times and you get to the point where your mind is calm, you may decide to:

1. **Focus on solving a problem or letting go of a particular worry.** When you do this, focus on one thing at a time and keep it simple.

2. **Send lots of love to the situation and trust that the outcome will resolve itself in a positive way.**

- **When you have finished**, blow out the candle and close your eyes, and notice the thoughts that come to you at this time. You will feel refreshed and relaxed and you may find you get some inspiration on what to do next.

You can use this meditation before you go to sleep, as it will relax you and clear your head.

'The Answer can help you master your own mind and avoid much of the fear and worry that permeates the world we live in.'

SUMMARY

- *The Answer* can help you master your own mind and avoid much of the fear and worry that permeates the world we live in.

- Most of the things you feared last week or last year won't have actually happened. Worrying was a complete waste of energy.

- When you're feeling fear, do what you can, send love to the situation and meditate on a positive outcome. Then let go of it.

- Use the techniques you learnt in *The Answer* to keep your focus positive and work on new goals. Try not to get bogged down in fear and worry.

- Focus on generating love to yourself and others. Love is the most powerful force in the Universe and will always overcome darkness.

- To calm your mind and alleviate fear, worry and stress use the *releasing fear and worry meditation* on page 176.

Joy

16

The Future

'I like the dreams of the future better than the history of the past.'

THOMAS JEFFERSON

Feeling insecure about the future can be a cause of stress. However, when it comes to the Law of Attraction, this kind of pessimism is counterproductive as you will unconsciously create situations that mirror your inner most beliefs.

I hope that *The Answer* has helped give you a more positive, optimistic perspective on life overall, particularly in chapter 7's Top Tips on Positive Thinking.

As you have discovered over the course of this book, with a little effort, it is easy to create a very positive outlook.

The things you do now will go towards creating your future. So developing a positive outlook is very important.

In this final chapter, I will give you some further techniques to help you stride confidently towards the future.

The future is golden

> *'The greatest discovery of all time is that a person can change his future by merely changing his attitude.'*
>
> OPRAH WINFREY

To create a positive future you have to believe your future is golden in the first place.

Even if things are not how you want them to be now, you can always change your future.

You do this not through hoping, wishing or yearning, which is weak and ineffective, but through positive visualisation and projecting beliefs that your future will be everything you want it to be.

> *'It is said that the present is pregnant with the future.'*
>
> VOLTAIRE

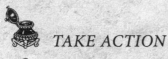 *TAKE ACTION*

Step into your future exercise

This exercise helps you to connect with your future in a positive way and can be used at any time of the day to remind yourself of what you are working towards.

- **Find somewhere that you won't be disturbed** and make yourself comfortable, either sitting or lying down. Then close your eyes.

- **Take a couple of deep breaths**.

- **Allow your mind to drift to somewhere peaceful** where everything is calm. A beach or pleasant garden for example. Spend a few minutes noticing what you can see in this place and also what you can hear and feel. Absorb yourself completely in this beautiful and calm place.

- **Next, imagine a path** and begin to walk along it, until you come to a large mirror.

- **In the reflection in the mirror, see yourself in the future** having achieved your goals and living the life of your dreams. Notice how happy this future self looks and what you are doing, saying and so on. Really connect with this future self and the positive feelings.

- **Step into the mirror, into your future self and experience how it feels** to have everything you want. Enjoy it and know that this is becoming your reality now. Stay here for as long as you want and then open your eyes whenever you feel ready.

Try it standing up

If you would prefer, you can do this exercise in a conscious state standing up.

- Imagine your future self standing in front of you; notice how the future you stands and holds him/herself as well as how they talk and look. Then step into your future self, taking on these qualities.

- Hold yourself as they hold themselves, talk as they talk and act as though you really are that future self now in the present moment. Acting as if you have all you want right now in the present moment will help you to attract it much more easily.

A change of scene

> '*Real generosity toward the future*
> *lies in giving all to the present.*'

ALBERT CAMUS

If you are feeling stuck, or in a rut, get away. Go where you will get a complete change of scenery. Visit somewhere that will inspire you and help you to feel more positive. Maybe it's wild and beautiful places that inspire you or places with a lot of culture and history.

If your budget and schedule is tight take a weekend trip locally and stay in a B&B or go camping. Or if you have more time and money, go further afield on a longer adventure to a place you've always wanted to visit.

Going forward

Remember, you always have a choice and the ability to change things and move forward. Taking action and being creative is the key to staying positive.

It is important to move forward in your life and to have things to look forward to.

Make a point of having events in your immediate future that you are looking forward to going to. These can be trips to the theatre, cinema, opera, sporting events or shows of any kind.

Having lots of things on the horizon will help you to move forward and give your life momentum.

Appreciate what you have

As you look ahead towards the future, remember that there are many things in your life worth valuing. Appreciating what you do have in every sense – family, a home, friends, your health, food and clothes – will help you to feel more fortunate.

Continue to be thankful and feel blessed for the good things in your daily life.

The importance of gratitude for what you already have is a subject I talk more about on page 85. The exercise opposite will encourage you to see with a fresh perspective.

'To create a positive future
you have to believe your future
is golden in the first place.'

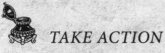

TAKE ACTION
A fresh perspective technique

- **Close your eyes and imagine this is your first day on Earth.**

- **Look around at all the things you have in your life.** You can see a home that keeps you sheltered and warm. Maybe you have the use of a car that gets you around? You have money to buy food and clothes and there are lots of shops for you to buy them from.

- **You see that there are people here who you love and who love you.** Continue to explore and acknowledge all the good things in your life now.

- **When you look at everything in your life you can feel very grateful for these blessings.** Focus on this feeling and continue to look at all the positives in your life now.

- **Connect with a feeling of happiness and joy.**

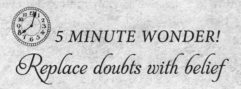

5 MINUTE WONDER!

Replace doubts with belief

Whenever an element of doubt creeps in while thinking of goals or when you are doing any kind of manifesting imagine a large red stop sign and banish that negative thought or self-doubt.

Then turn the negative phrase in your head into a positive one. Accept that you deserve all the good life has to offer...and believe it!

This is very important as if you don't think you deserve it the Universe will think the same.

You are what you feel – so feel good and deserving at all times.

SUMMARY

- The things you do now will go towards creating your future so developing a positive outlook is very important.

- To create a positive future you have to believe your future is golden in the first place.

- To connect with your future in a positive way try the *step into your future* exercise (see page 183).

- If you are feeling stuck, or in a rut, try a change of scenery.

- It is important to move forward in your life and to have things to look forward to.

- As you look ahead towards the future, don't forget to appreciate and feel gratitude for all the good things in your daily life.

- Remember to turn negative phrases in your head into positive ones. Accept that you deserve all the good life has to offer.

'I am not afraid. . .
I was born to do this'.

JOAN OF ARC

The Answer:
12 Golden Rules

'You may say I'm a dreamer, but I'm not the only one. I hope someday you'll join us. And the World will live as one.'

JOHN LENNON

Golden rule 1

Believe you are successful NOW. You need to create a thought process whereby every cell in your mind and body believes that you are already successful – even if you are not at this moment. When you create the belief that you have achieved your goal, opportunity will come knocking and the reality will soon manifest itself.

*

Golden rule 2

Mind your language at all times. Avoid talking about things you don't like or are unhappy with. Always talk about what you like and what you love.

Golden rule 3

Show gratitude for all the good things in your life. Whenever you meditate start with giving thanks for all the blessings in your life.

*

Golden rule 4

Believe with every cell and fibre in your mind body and spirit that you DESERVE to be happy, successful and abundant. This is your divine right, so accept it as normal and natural.

Golden rule 5

Get into the habit of using the Law Of Attraction as often as possible so that it becomes a normal part of your everyday thinking.

*

Golden rule 6

Keep your orders positive. The Universe doesn't interpret negatives well. Always focus on what you do want and not what you don't want and be crystal clear when setting your goals as you will attract exactly what you project.

Golden rule 7

Apply the 80/20 rule to everything in your life. Aim to stay healthy, be positive, avoid being critical, exercise often, work towards your goal and be disciplined but don't expect to be perfect in everything you do. Set your goals high and aim for success 80 per cent of the time. If you make errors or fall off the wagon 20 per cent of the time then you are doing okay.

Golden rule 8

Let go of attachment to material possessions and outcomes. Liberate yourself by setting goals, using the Law of Attraction to manifest them and then letting them go. Do not take ownership of anything just accept everything as it is.

Golden rule 9

Do not discuss your goals and aims with other people. Idle chatter can dissipate the energy you build. Go forward in a silent and disciplined way building your inner strength and energy through meditation.

Golden rule 10

Enjoy your life and laugh a lot! Laughing and joking with people is a wonderful way to communicate and to build a rapport. People like to be around others who are fun and make them laugh.

If there is not enough fun and laughter in your life then work on this consciously. Develop the art of being light-hearted and having fun.

Golden rule 11

Spread the love! Practise being big hearted, loving and kind to yourself and others and always be generous with your words and time. Project unconditional love from your heart towards everyone you come into contact with, even strangers who walk past you in the street. The more love you give the more it will come into your life. This rule alone can transform your life.

*

Golden rule 12

Live your life in the present moment at all times, and avoid excessive thoughts of the past or future. Being present and connected to the now will help you manifest things more easily. When your mind is focused in the present moment your creativity and inspiration will flow.

TAKE ACTION

To download Glenn Harrold's powerful new
Law of Attraction hypnosis tracks, scan the
code below* or go to the Orion website:
www.orionbooks.co.uk/promotions/the-answer